CORVETTE
AMERICA'S SPORTS CAR

BY THE EDITORS OF CONSUMER GUIDE® AUTOMOTIVE

Publications International, Ltd.

Louis Weber, CEO
Publications International, Ltd.
7373 North Cicero Avenue
Lincolnwood, Illinois 60712

ISBN-13: 978-1-4508-2688-4
ISBN-10: 1-4508-2688-1

Manufactured in China.

8 7 6 5 4 3 2 1

Library of Congress Control Number: 2011925348

Credits

Photography

The editors would like to thank the following people and organizations for supplying the photography that made this book possible. They are listed below, along with the page number(s) of their photos:

Mark Bilek: 144, 145; **Jeff Cohn:** 186, 187; **Mitch Frumkin:** 128, 129, 134; **Thomas Glatch:** 13, 14, 50, 51; **Sam Griffith:** 62, 63, 122, 123, 126, 127, 142, 143, 156, 157; **Bud Juneau:** 36, 37, 48, 49, 110, 111; **Gary Kessler:** 100, 101; **Milton Kieft:** 38, 39, 54, 55; **Lloyd Koenig:** 35; **Nick Komic:** 94, 95; **Dan Lyons:** 58, 59; **Vince Manocchi:** 14, 15, 17, 26, 27, 28, 52, 53, 68, 69, 78, 79, 80, 81, 82, 83, 88, 89, 96, 97, 102, 103, 132, 133; **Roger Mattingly:** 180, 181; **Ron McQueeney:** 28; **Doug Mitchel:** 29, 31, 32, 33, 64, 65, 76, 77, 158, 159, 162, 163, 164, 165, 166, 167, 168, 169; **Mike Mueller:** 23; **Neil Nissing:** 149, 160, 161; **Nina Padgett:** 84, 85, 146, 147, 154, 155; **Richard Spiegelmen:** 92, 93; **Tom Storm:** 18, 19; **David Temple:** 6, 7, 56, 57, 136, 137; **Phil Toy:** 19, 130, 131; **W. C. Waymack:** 86, 87

Front Cover: Ron Kimball/www.kimballstock.com

Owners

Special thanks to the owners of the cars featured in this book for their cooperation. Their names and the page number(s) for their vehicles follow:

Mark Alter: 88, 89; **Howard L. Baker:** 54, 55; **Les Bieri and John Angwert:** 13; **James Buie Jr.:** 136, 137; **Dorothy Clemmer:** 14, 15, 96, 97; **Patrick and Kay Collins:** 82, 83; **Corvette Mike:** 132, 133; **Allen Cummins:** 68, 69; **George Don-Pedro:** 130, 131; **John M. Endres:** 110, 111; **David L. Ferguson:** 17; **Gateway Classic Cars:** 86, 87; **Jack Gersh:** 80, 81; **Gary A. Girt:** 38, 39; **Eric P. Goodman:** 32; **Russ Hibbs:** 94, 95; **J. Bruce Jacobs:** 52, 53; **John E. and Barbara James:** 84, 85; **JMPR:** 35; **Bill Jones:** 36, 37; **Roger Judski:** 116, 117; **Arnold Kaplan:** 31; **Robert Kleckauskas:** 62, 63; **Barry L. Klinkel:** 78, 79; **Edward S Kuziel:** 23; **Rich Mason:** 28; **Werner Meier:** 50, 51; **Don Mershon:** 100, 101; **Edward E. Ortiz:** 102, 103; **Dr. Dennis Pagliano:** 26, 27; **Robert Paterson:** 48, 49; **Jim Patterson:** 64, 65; **Pro Team Corvette Sales:** 29; **Danny Reed:** 6, 7, 56, 57; **RM Classic Cars:** 19; **Alfred W. Schwacke:** 18, 19; **Forrest Shropshire:** 22; **Phil Trifaro:** 58, 59; **Mike and Laurie Yager:** 76, 77

Our appreciation to the historical archives and media services groups at General Motors Company.

CONTENTS

FOREWORD

Despite chill, rainy weather in New York City on January 17, 1953, crowds thronged General Motors's '53 Motorama show. Before the doors opened on that Saturday morning, lines outside the Waldorf-Astoria Hotel stretched along Park Avenue to Fiftieth Street, up to Lexington Avenue, and on Lexington all the way to Fifty-first.

First-day attendance topped 45,000, and although GM was showing some 135 exhibits of automobiles and products, visitors were particularly excited by Chevrolet's EX-122, a sleek, low-slung roadster that Chevrolet had named "Corvette," to evoke small, maneuverable, and powerful naval ships of World War II.

During the show's first day, *The New York Times* asked GM design chief Harley Earl to comment on the Corvette's novel use of fiberglass. He said, "From the styling standpoint we believe we have entered a new and interesting field."

What an understatement.

So warm was the public reaction to the Motorama Corvette that the first production example rolled off the assembly line on June 30, hardly more than five months later. And except for some trim pieces, the production car was essentially unchanged from the concept.

For the next five decades and counting, shapely fiberglass Corvette bodies became iconic on America's roadways. And after dramatic improvement to Corvette powertrains for 1955, the cars became known for booming power. Before Corvette was ten years old, it had become as close to a legend as a thing can be.

With that first generation, and with the subsequent Sting Ray and "Shark" and the C4, all the way to special, carbon-fiber-edition C6s, Corvette has meant considerably more than transportation. It means innovation and excitement, sophistication and blunt force, and world-class performance at reasonable prices.

It is as intriguingly contradictory as the nation that birthed it. It is America's Sports Car.

Corvette burst onto the American auto scene with a hugely well-received debut at the 1953 Motorama. The first production Corvettes, though stylish, were underpowered. Greatness came a little later.

1953–1962: GROWING TOWARD GREATNESS

The Corvette was born of America's early-1950s boom economy, a heady time when anything seemed possible, especially for General Motors. Having grown to become the world's largest automaker by far, GM dominated the U.S. market and thus virtually industry design, engineering, and pricing trends. Much of the company's success was owed to Harley Earl, who established Detroit's first in-house styling department—the "Art & Colour" studio—and invented the "dream car" (today's "concept car") as both publicity tool and testbed. The Corvette was merely Chevrolet's dream for the 1953 edition of GM's annual Motorama show. Staged between 1949 and 1961, the Motoramas were lavish spectacles that toured the country to promote the company's latest wares and gauge showgoers' response to ideas for future models.

For as long as the Motorama shows existed, no expense was spared to make them consumer-friendly and publicity-ready. GM had the lion's share of the U.S. auto market during the Fifties, but extra exposure in newspapers and on television was always welcomed. To that end, the Motoramas gave employment to small armies of dancers, musicians, and other performers. Good-looking female models also were put to work, complementing the cars and various other product displays.

It was in this highly charged, big-money, show-biz atmosphere that the concept Corvette first greeted its public.

Though Harley Earl favored flashy aircraft-inspired design, he admired clean, athletic European sports cars designed for maximum driving pleasure, not just A-to-B transportation. Seeing that sports cars were starting to capture the public imagination, and mindful of Chevrolet's then-stodgy brand image, Earl pushed for an affordable, all-American sports car wearing the bowtie badge.

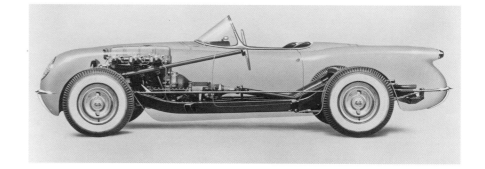

The result premiered in January 1953 after a 30-month collaboration between Earl's team and the Chevrolet Division Engineering Staff. Enthusiastic response prompted GM management to okay production—a brave decision, as sports cars then accounted for less than one percent of total U.S. car sales. Though the show car (Project EX-122) had been developed mainly to make a deadline, engineers productionized the design with remarkable speed, and the first Corvette came off a small assembly line at Chevy's Flint, Michigan, plant on June 30, 1953.

Opposite: Corvette had a powerful patron in GM design chief Harley Earl. Although the car's mechanicals were far from groundbreaking, the Motorama Corvette—which changed almost not at all for production—was low and strikingly handsome. *Right:* Each 'Vette required considerable hand labor on the Flint assembly line.

All Corvettes through 1962 rode a 102-inch wheelbase, a dimension shared with the Jaguar XK-120, one of Earl's favorite sports cars. The Motorama Corvette employed a modified Chevrolet passenger-car frame, but the production chassis ended up virtually all-new. The chassis design was conventional, with front coil springs and double A-arms, a solid rear axle on semi-elliptic leaf springs, and unassisted recirculating-ball steering and drum brakes. Body construction was quite daring, however, marking the first use of fiberglass in a regular production car by a major automaker. Fiberglass was attractive because it could be molded into more-complex shapes than steel stampings—which appealed to the designers—and because it was more cost-effective for a low-volume model—which appealed to GM accountants. No less important, it did not compromise crash safety. Styling was typical period Harley Earl: rounded,

Opposite, far left: Nine major sub-assemblies of the Corvette's body were comprised of 46 separate pieces glued together. *Left, top:* As the first-generation Corvette acquired more power and better road manners, factory-sponsored racing and competition R&D grew increasingly important. *Left, center:* A proposed Corvette wagon, the Nomad, was a 1954 dream car. Although never produced, it inspired the '55 Chevy Nomad wagon. *This page:* A low stance, a stylish cockpit and reasonably utilitarian dash, stone guards, and Polo White—always—helped define the '53 Corvette.

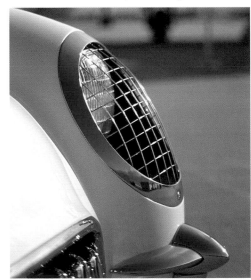

low, and "futuristic," with extended pod-type taillights, a toothy grille, trendy wraparound windshield, and Euro-style wire-mesh covers for the headlamps.

Ironically, in view of what lay ahead, the Corvette almost expired after 1955 due to very low sales. Just 315 were built for '53 (most reserved for promotion and favored VIPs), followed by 3640 for '54—when production was moved to St. Louis—and a mere 700 of the '55s. Some blamed this disappointing performance on the car's rather odd mix of features.

Boulevardier types disliked the British-style plastic side curtains, clumsy manual-fold cloth top, and the lack of both a back seat and exterior door handles. Enthusiasts chided the gimmicky looks and a plodding drivetrain that married Chevy's two-speed Powerglide automatic transmission with the division's elderly 235.5-cubic-inch "Blue Flame" six. Still, the Corvette engine was treated to triple carburetors, high-lift camshaft, higher compression, and other changes that upped horsepower from 115 to 150—respectable for the day—and the car's 2700-pound curb weight.

Both pages: Today, two- and three-car families are common, but in 1953, when new homes were still built with one-car garages, the notion of a second car struck many Americans as frivolous. In that kind of environment, the Corvette wasn't just a sports car, but a true luxury. The hardy but uninspired Blue Flame six gave non-sporting performance (turning off driving enthusiasts), but the total package was too snug and quirky to be a daily driver, which made the 'Vette a nonstarter with "everyday" buyers.

Thanks to pleas from Earl and Chevy chief engineer Ed Cole (left), GM decided in late 1954 to give Corvette a second chance. And Cole had what would prove to be the car's salvation: the brilliant 265-cid overhead-valve V-8 that he'd designed with Harry Barr, John Gordon, and others for Chevy's all-new 1955 passenger cars. Arriving with 195 hp, the V-8 vastly improved performance, cutting 0–60-mph acceleration by more than two seconds, to 8.7. No wonder it was installed in all but seven of the '55 Corvettes built. A newly optional three-speed floorshift manual gearbox also helped transform the

FORECAST OF A NEW ERA

IN AMERICAN SPORTS CARS...

The Corvette

BY CHEVROLET

MASTERFUL AUTOMOBILE STYLING BY THE SALES LEADER . . . CHEVROLET

Powered by an advanced "Blue Flame" engine, the Corvette develops 150 horsepower from an overhead-valve, six cylinder engine. Equipped with the newest Powerglide automatic transmission. Specifications: two seater; 33 inches high; 70 inches wide; 167 inches length; 2900 pounds curb weight.

CHEVROLET

THE FIRST ALL-AMERICAN SPORTS CAR IN PRODUCTION

Opposite: In an inspired stroke of marketing and promotion, a pride of '54 Corvettes negotiated the infamous S-curve of Chicago's Lake Shore Drive. Cars traveling in the opposite direction inevitably looked staid by comparison. *This page:* A bit more than 3600 Corvettes were produced for 1954. Changes were negligible. The car looked fabulous in black, and the windshield was dramatically wrapped, but the inadequate six carried on as the sole engine.

car's image from "plastic bathtub" to serious sporting machine. Even so, Chevrolet had 1100 unsold '54s at the start of '55 production, which hampered sales in spite of the many improvements.

The '56 Corvette was improved almost beyond recognition, and Chevy rightly proclaimed it "America's only true sports car." A rounded rump and beautifully sculpted bodysides with curving, concave "coves," just aft of the front-wheel openings, marked a stunning change from the slab-sided original. Convenient roll-up windows and an optional lift-off

Opposite and this page, top and top right: Only 700 Corvettes were built for 1955, but they all ran with Chevy's new small-block V-8 that displaced 265 cubic inches and developed 195 horsepower. *Above and*

right: Euro-styling distinguishes this one-off gran turismo combination of '54 'Vette chassis and powertrain with an aluminum body by Ghia. It was designed by Giovanni Michellotti.

hardtop (both previewed on 1954 Motorama specials) made motoring more civilized, as did pushbutton door handles outside. Sensibly, Chevy now dropped the old six and retuned the V-8 for 210 or 225 hp (the latter via a high-lift camshaft, twin four-barrel carburetors, and dual exhausts),

Opposite and this page, bottom: Racing success came at Daytona in 1956. Production cars could be had with a semi-automatic power-operated top that was a $170.60 option. *Right:* The Corvette SR-2 was built in 1956 for Harley Earl's son, Jerry. The car had a longer snout than the production Corvette, a toothier grille, twin windscreens, and a hard-to-miss, faired-in fin and headrest combo. In 1957, the SR-2 made good showings at the Daytona Speed Weeks and at Sebring. Because Chevy put together a second SR-2, the one seen here is commonly referred to as the "racing" SR-2, or the "Jerry Earl car."

PEBBLE BEACH
Production Car Race, Over 1500 c.c

1st in Class C – CORVETTE
2nd Over-all – CORVETTE

FINISH

The 1956 Corvette is proving — in open competition — that it is America's only genuine production sports car. Extremely stable, with outrigger leaf springs at the rear, 16 to 1 steering ratio and weight distribution close to 50-50, it has demonstrated its ability to corner on equal terms with the best European production sports cars. Of particular interest to the competition driver are the close-ratio manual gearbox, with 2.2 to 1 low gear and 1.11 to 1 second gear; the two rear axle ratios of 3.70 to 1 or 3.27 to 1; the power-to-weight advantage of the Corvette's glass fiber body and the special racing brake lining, now available at Chevrolet dealerships.

Mainspring of the Corvette's per-formance is, of course, the fantastically efficient 4.3-litre V8 Chevrolet engine. Holder of the Pikes Peak stock car record, heart of the Corvette that set a two-way American mark of 150 m.p.h. at Daytona Beach last January, powerplant of the NASCAR stock car Short Track champion, this short-stroke V8 is capable of turning well over 5000 r.p.m. The Corvette makes it available in two versions: 210 h.p. with the single four-barrel carburetor, and 225 h.p. with dual four-barrel carburetors. A special high-performance cam is optional at extra cost.

For the driver who requires a superlative touring car rather than a competition machine the Corvette is available with such extra-cost lux-uries as removable hardtop, power-operated cloth top and window lifters, plus the Powerglide automatic transmission. And, for either choice, there is the assurance of reasonably priced service and parts at any of nearly 7500 Chevrolet dealerships.

If you are considering a sports car, don't fail to sample the 1956 Corvette. It is the surprise car of the year, as your Chevrolet dealer will be delighted to demonstrate.

CHEVROLET

CORVETTE

which made performance even more thrilling. Adept chassis changes by newly hired engineer Zora Arkus-Duntov made handling even more capable. The close-ratio three-speed manual replaced Powerglide as the standard transmission; the automatic moved to the options sheet. The most-potent '56 could nail 60 mph from rest in just 7.5 seconds and top 120 miles per hour.

Opposite: Modified stock Corvettes did well in competition by the late Fifties. In 1986, Forrest Shropshire piloted a 1956 'Vette—with some handmade aerodynamic mods—to 180 mph at Bonneville Salt Flats. *This page:* For 1956, Corvette sales bounced upward to 3467 units—enough to ensure that the car wouldn't be canceled. But it had been a close call. The '56 'Vette was fully refreshed with a more capable chassis, an optional lift-off hardtop, and roll-up windows. The six, which had still been available for 1955, was dropped altogether a year later; output of the V-8 was increased to 210 and 225 horsepower. Manual transmission was standard, and a Corvette now could zip from 0 to 60 mph in 7.5 seconds.

There was no need to change the handsome styling for 1957, but Chevy again upped performance by boring out the V-8 to 283 cid. The enlarged engine came in five versions offering 220 hp up to an amazing 283, the latter courtesy of new "Ramjet" fuel injection. A four-speed manual transmission arrived in April at $188 extra, and combined with axle ratios as low as 4.56:1 to make "fuelie" '57s thunderously fast. Published road tests showed 0–60 in 5.7 seconds, 0–100 mph in 16.8 seconds, the standing quarter-mile in 14.3 seconds at 96 mph, and a maximum speed of 132-plus mph. Unfortunately, mechanical bugs and a steep $500 price limited Ramjet installations to only 1040 units that model year. Chevy also offered a $725 "heavy-duty racing suspension" with high-rate springs and shocks, front antiroll bar, quick steering, and metallic brake linings with finned drums. With this and one of the high-power engines, a '57 'Vette was virtually ready to race right off the showroom floor.

Opposite: In 1956, Chevy general manager (and ace engineer) Ed Cole knew that no modified stock Corvette would ever win outright at the 12 Hours of Endurance at Sebring. Original Corvette engineer Zora Arkus-Duntov (white hair) lent his considerable expertise to the creation of what came to be called the Corvette Super Sport (SS). The XP-64 program was unusually ambitious, but brought mixed results.

This page: The Corvette V-8 was enlarged to 283 cubic inches for 1957. Two of five available versions had Ramjet fuel injection with 250 or 283 hp—and that was the magic "1 hp per cu. in." This '57, with removable hardtop in place, is a small masterpiece of visual understatement.

And indeed, Corvette now began making its mark in international competition. Dr. Richard Thompson won the Sports Car Club of America (SCCA) C-Production national championship in 1956, then took the '57 crown in B-Production, where the 'Vette qualified because of its larger V-8. John Fitch's '56 was the fastest modified car at that year's Daytona Speed Weeks, a Corvette finished ninth in the grueling 12 Hours of Sebring in '56, and another came home second at Pebble Beach. A bold 1957 assault on the fabled Sebring 12-Hour race in Florida saw production Corvettes finish 1–2 in the GT class and 12th and 15th overall.

Such successes symbolized a dramatic metamorphosis. Said one European auto writer: "Before Sebring…the Corvette was regarded as a plastic toy. After Sebring, even the most biased were forced to admit that [it was] one of the world's finest sports cars…." The public happily responded to this package, buying 3467 of the '56s and 6339 of the '57s. Corvette's future was assured.

Opposite right, top two photos: Inspired originally by the D-Type racing Jaguar, the SS eventually came to look very much like the production '56 Corvette. Although extensively tested, it was a competition disappointment. *Opposite, other photos:* Various iterations of the SR-2. *This page: Road & Track* noted that the 283 fuelie's best attribute was "its instantaneous throttle response." This is a '57.

Seeking even higher sales, Chevy redesigned the Corvette for 1958. The result was a busier, shinier sports car measuring 10 inches longer and more than two inches wider. Yet despite that and a huskier look, it was only a few pounds heavier than the 1956–57 models. The basic shape was broadly the same except for quad headlamps (all the rage that year), a dummy air scoop ahead of each bodyside "cove," simulated hood louvers, and equally silly chrome strips down the trunklid. Yet there were genuine improvements, including sturdier bumpers and a redesigned cockpit with passenger grab bar, locking glovebox, and all instruments grouped ahead of the driver (instead of spread across the dash). Performance remained vivid because engines were little changed for '58. In fact, the top fuel-injected 283 gained seven horsepower to reach 290, thus exceeding the hallowed "1 hp per cu. in." benchmark achieved the previous year.

Inflation plagued the national economy in '58, cutting deeply into sales of most Detroit cars. Yet Corvette was one of the few to buck the

Both pages: Model-year 1958 was a chrome-heavy one for GM cars, so we all should be thankful that the freshened '58 Corvette wasn't tarted up more than it was. The grille was now flanked by dummy air scoops, and the bodyside coves sported new—and fake—air vents. Quad headlamps had come into vogue and were the starting point for chrome strips that described the fender tops. Strangest of all (though perhaps a nod to Classic-era boots) was a pair of decorative chrome strips that longitudinally bisected the deck. All three Corvette engines for '58 displaced 283 cubic inches. In standard form, the mill produced 230 horsepower. An optional, carbureted variant had 245 or 270 hp, while the top engine (shown) was an efficient, fuel-injected unit that cranked out 250 or, as here, 290 horses.

trend. A still-reasonable base price helped: $3631, up just $118 versus debut '53. Critics generally liked the '58. So did buyers. Model-year production rose to 9168 units, up 2829 over the '57 tally, and Corvette turned a profit for the first time.

Volume rose by another 500 units for '59, to 9670. Few changes occurred, but enthusiasts applauded as Chevy smoothed out the hood, deleted the chrome trunk trim, and added trailing radius rods (the one notable technical change) to counteract rear-axle windup in hard acceleration.

This basic package carried into 1960 as Corvette production passed the magic 10,000 mark for the first time (by 261 units). That year brought a larger 24-gallon fuel tank as a new extra, and the optional heavy-duty suspension was replaced by a larger front antiroll bar and a new standard rear bar. An extra inch of wheel travel in rebound further contributed to more-neutral handling, as well as a smoother ride. Aluminum radiators were newly available, but announced cast-aluminum cylinder heads didn't make it.

Though Corvette was quickly evolving from *pur sang* sports car to plush *grand turismo,* it remained a formidable track competitor. Highlights in this period include a GT-class win and 12th overall at Sebring '58, SCCA B-Production national championships in 1958 and 1959, fastest sports car at the 1958 Pikes Peak Hill Climb, and a slew of victories by privateers. Thanks to a mid-1957 agreement among members of the Automobile Manufacturers Association, Chevy was officially "out of racing" now, but not above lending under-the-table support to those campaigning its cars. Among them was sportsman Briggs Cunningham, who gave Corvette one of its finest racing hours when one of his three team cars (driven by John Fitch and Bob Grossman) finished eighth in the 1960 running of the fabled 24 Hours of Le Mans.

The 1960 Corvette might have been a very different animal. Beginning in 1957, Chevy contemplated a smaller, lighter sports car based on the prototype "Q-model," with a rear transaxle, independent rear suspension, and inboard disc brakes. A full-size mockup ultimately took shape bearing a remarkable resemblance to the production Sting Ray then six years distant, but the project was abandoned because of the '58 recession and the time and money being expended to bring out Chevy's rear-engine 1960 Corvair compact.

Opposite: Corvette dumped some of the chrome gingerbread for 1959, and the revised design carried on virtually unchanged for 1960 (shown). But now the top fuelie V-8 produced a hairy-chested 315 hp. The power was handled by a much-improved suspension. *This page, clockwise from bottom left:* Despite losing some chrome for 1960, the Corvette still had a flashy, glittery face and body. Performance, though, continued to improve. A prototype '58 sits proudly outside the GM styling center. Lastly, designer Bill Mitchell's XP-700 show car of 1958 suggested one possible Corvette. A Mitchell mantra went, "You need two things in a car. You need road value and showroom value. You need a little sparkle in a car."

There was nothing to do but soldier on with the existing Corvette while designers and engineers devised a less-radical replacement. Meantime, Harley Earl retired as GM design chief in 1958, and his successor, William L. Mitchell, breathed new life into the three-year-old styling.

The result was a 1961 Corvette that was "tail lifted" aft of the doors along the lines of Mitchell's 1959 Stingray racer (built on the "mule" chassis salvaged from 1957's unsuccessful Corvette SS prototype effort at Sebring and campaigned privately). The new flowing "ducktail" not only increased luggage space by some 20 percent but mated handsomely with the 1958–60 front, which Mitchell simplified by substituting mesh for the familiar chrome grille "teeth."

Opposite, top and lower right: The 1959 Corvette Stingray Special was built on the '57 Sebring "mule" chassis and competed, with little success, on the SCCA C Sports Racing class in '59. Things were better in 1960, when the car won the national class championship. Here, Corvette driver Dr. Dick Thompson is pursued by Max Balchowsky's Old Yeller II, a very capable homebuilt racer that gave other cars fits. *Opposite, lower left:* The 1961 Shark show car was developed from ideas first explored two years earlier on the XP-700. *This page:* Zora Arkus-Duntov's CERV-I racer was designed to compete at Indianapolis—never mind that a corporate racing ban was in effect. In trials at Daytona, the 1450-pound CERV averaged 206 mph. Arkus-Duntov's CERV-II was a closed-body follow-on conceived in 1962.

Horsepower for the top fuelie V-8 jumped to 315 for '61 (other engines stood pat), and Chevy added new refinements: standard sunvisors, a higher-capacity aluminum-core radiator, side-mount expansion tanks, and a wider choice of axle ratios. Base price was up to $3934, but that dough got you a lot of go. Even the mildest 230-hp 283 with Powerglide was good for 7.7 seconds 0–60 mph and nearly 110 mph flat out; figures for the 315-hp mill with four-speed manual were 5.5 seconds and 130-plus mph. In case anyone still doubted Corvette's track prowess, a near-stock model finished 11th at Sebring in '61 against much-costlier and more-exotic racing machinery.

Both pages: Model-year 1961 brought a new ducktail rear end that gave additional luggage space. Chrome was trimmed back this year. The small, round taillights were new, as well, and gave a hint of what the all-new '63 units would be. Dual exhausts now exited separately, rather than through the body or bumper, as in the past. For a bit of drama, a longitudinal crease appeared on the trunk lid. Up front, a horizontal-mesh design meant a newly understated grille. There was little standard equipment for the year; even a heater was a $102 option. Engines were unchanged from 1960, with the hardy 283 producing 230, 245, 270, 275, and 315 horsepower.

Refinement was again the keynote for '62, but Chevy gave a hint of things to come by offering the next Corvette's engines in what would be the last of the "solid-axle" models (now referred to as the "C1" generation). There were four of them, one fuelie and three with carburetors; all were 283s that were bored-and-stroked to 327 cid. Horsepower ranged from 250 to a thumping 360. The fuel-injection system was modified for greater reliability, a new 3.08:1 final-drive ratio gave quieter cruising with the two lowest-power engines, and the heavy-duty suspension option was reinstated from '59. Styling was cleaner than ever. Mitchell eliminated the chrome outline around the "coves" and their optional two-toning, blacked-in the grille, and added ribbed-aluminum appliqués to rocker panels and the dummy reverse front-fender scoops.

Corvette continued its winning ways on the track and in the showroom for '62. Dick Thompson, the "flying dentist," won that year's national A-Production crown in SCCA, Don Yenko the B-P title. More important to GM managers, production was still climbing, from 1961's record 10,000-plus to 14,531.

In all, the Corvette came a long way in its first 10 years, maturing rapidly from auto-show exercise into one of the world's most respected sports cars. A new American icon had been born, but its story was just beginning.

Both pages: Chevy was eager to bring an all-new Corvette generation to market but stuck with the familiar for one more season, 1962. The most exciting news was the new standard engine, a 283 bored out to 327 cid, with 250, 300, 340, and 360 horsepower. With the top fuelie 327, a '62 Corvette could race from 0 to 60 mph in 5.9 seconds—a dazzling figure. On the body, chrome trim was finally abandoned on the side coves, which no longer had discrete colors. The grille mesh was now painted black rather than chromed. A heater was finally standard equipment. Factory air and power brakes were optional. The detachable hardtop remained available, priced now at $236.75. And for the first time, the base price of a Corvette topped $4000 at $4038.

Corvette convertibles were always gorgeous, but had there ever been a coupe to match the beauty of the '63 Sting Ray? Subsequent models were nearly as pretty, and 'Vette just got faster and more capable.

1963–1967: THIS STING RAY BITES!

Seldom has a car changed more in one model year than Corvette did for 1963. Apart from four wheels and two seats, about the only things the new Sting Ray had in common with the final "C1" models were fiberglass bodywork and a 327 V-8 in "front midships" positioning. Most everything else was different, underscored by the addition of a sleek fastback-coupe body style.

The 1961–62 Corvette had been a satisfying and successful conclusion to the design generation begun with the '56 model (or, to some eyes, as far back as the '53). But after all that time, the moment to move on had arrived, the moment to unveil the "all-new" Corvette that had been rumored off and on since 1958.

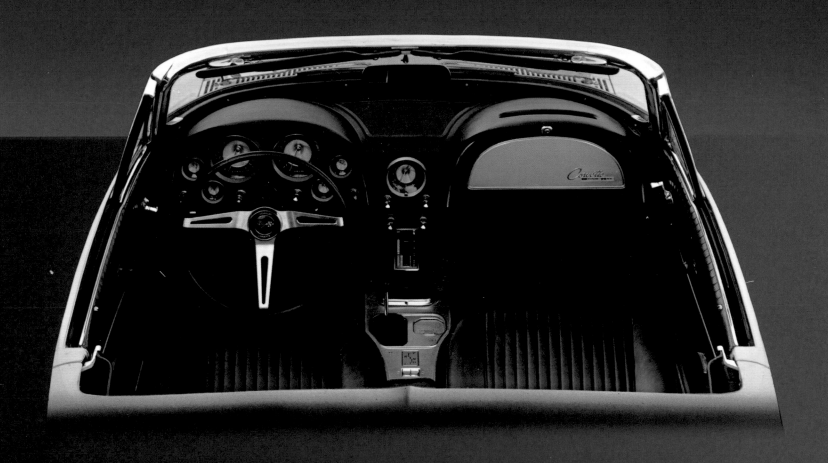

Like the 1961–62 Corvettes, the Sting Ray reflected the passion and corporate clout of General Motors design chief William L. Mitchell, Corvette chief engineer Zora Arkus-Duntov, and Edward N. Cole and Bunkie Knudsen, who headed Chevrolet Division during the car's development. Building on the experimental 1957 Q-Corvette effort and Mitchell's privateer Stingray racer of 1959–60, project XP-720 aimed to deliver a trimmer, lighter, safer, more-agile, and more-refined Chevy sports car with even better straightline performance and dazzling new looks. And so it did. Indeed, many enthusiasts still regard the "C2" as the best Corvette ever.

Though not immediately apparent, the Sting Ray was slightly shorter than its 1961–62 forebears and rode a four-inch-shorter wheelbase (at 98). It was also some 50 pounds lighter, thanks to a new ladder-type frame with five crossmembers—replacing the heavy old X-member affair—and despite

Opposite, top: During 1961, clay models of what would be the all-new 1963 Sting Ray were tested in the wind tunnel at Cal Tech. Opposite, bottom: GM design chief Bill Mitchell customized this Corvette for use by his legendary predecessor, Harley Earl. This page: The XP-720 was a running concept of a 2+2 intended to compete with Ford's Thunderbird. It was never built, and that's probably for the best.

a new steel upper-body "birdcage" that made for a stronger, safer cockpit. The Sting Ray used almost twice as much structural steel as previous 'Vettes, and less fiberglass.

The added rigidity was deemed necessary for the more-potent engines being planned for the future, but mainly because Duntov insisted on a fully independent rear suspension (irs) that would allow higher cornering forces than solid-axle 'Vettes ever knew. A first for a modern U.S. production car, the Sting Ray's irs employed a single transverse leaf spring attached to a frame-mounted differential whose U-jointed halfshafts acted as upper control arms. Lower arms ran laterally and slightly forward to the hub carriers to control vertical suspension movement. A pair of trailing radius rods fitted behind the diff limited fore/aft motion and transferred

braking torque to the frame. This arrangement was elegantly simple, relatively cheap, and highly effective, bringing a desirable reduction in unsprung weight.

Front/rear weight distribution improved from 53/47 percent to 48/52. Another boon to handling was higher-geared recirculating-ball steering with a hydraulic damper added and first-time-available power assist. Abetted by an updated dual-arm, three-link, ball-joint front suspension, the Sting Ray boasted quicker steering response and less kickback through the wheel. Drum brakes continued but now were self-adjusting, and the fronts were wider for increased swept area. With all this, Corvette ride and handling were better than ever.

Powertrains were basically '62 carryovers, but smaller flywheels

Champion-sparked cars rule the races at Riverside

Set up and entered by Mickey Thompson, a Champion-sparked Sting Ray Corvette wins the special 3-hour race! The Formula Junior race is won on Champions. And Champion-fired cars win both classes in the Grand Prix for Sports Cars, with 76,000 fans cheering on the top American and International sports car drivers at California's Riverside Raceway . . .

Mickey Thompson finds new speed worlds to conquer—and conquers them—in this Chevy Sting Ray Corvette beats a field of over 50 entries in the "Invitational 3-Hour Enduro" at Riverside Raceway. This was the first road-race competition for the new Corvettes, and the Champion-fired, Thompson-prepared Sting Ray, driven by Doug Hooper, covered 252.2 miles during the 3 hours, averaging 84.06 mph over the hills and curves of the 2.6-mile road racing course.

The 25-lap race for Formula Junior cars was won by Ed Leslie in the Champion-fired Lotus 22 Ford. Leslie is one of the country's top Formula Junior drivers, finishing second in 1962 SCCA Championship points for F2 drivers in the "west of the Rockies" division of the Sports Car Club of America.

Roger Penske took first over-all, and set a new race record of 96.6 mph in the fifth Riverside Grand Prix for Sports Cars. This 77-lap event covers 200.2 miles, with 33 top American and International sports car drivers starting. A week after Riverside, Penske and his Champion-sparked Cooper Special won the Pacific Grand Prix at Laguna Seca, putting Penske in first place in the North American Championship point standings.

Innes Ireland, one of the world's leading road-racing drivers, took first in the "under 2 liter" class of the Grand Prix, finishing 6th over-all and beating many bigger-bore machines with his Champion-sparked Lotus 19. In 1961, Ireland won the big Grand Prix of the United States on Champions.

Performance like this is more proof of a fact that engine experts have long known: No one has ever built a spark plug to out-perform a Champion! In 1962 sports car racing and drag racing—from Sebring to Riverside . . . from the Winternationals to the National Drags—it was proved again and again! So next time you install spark plugs, insist on the plugs that pack the performance punch—silvery-plated Champions!

DEPENDABLE **CHAMPION** SPARK PLUGS

CHAMPION SPARK PLUG COMPANY TOLEDO 1, OHIO

Opposite: Bill Mitchell emphasized the new Sting Ray's competition heritage by posing with it and the Stingray Racer. *This page, above:* A Sting Ray is a featured car in this 1963 spark plug advertisement. *Other photos:* Dating back more than six years, Corvettes found success at Sebring and in SCCA events. That kind of credibility made the car a natural choice for parts and aftermarket suppliers who wanted to associate their products with a winner. Pictured is the Corvette Grand Sport.

improved "revvability." Positive crankcase ventilation appeared as an early anti-pollution measure, and old-fashioned generators gave way to more-efficient alternators. As before, buyers could choose from four-barrel 327 V-8s tuned for 250, 300, and 340 horsepower, plus a top-dog fuel-injected version with 360 (and a steep $430 price). The base and step-up mills employed hydraulic lifters, mild camshaft profile, forged-steel crankshaft, 10.5:1 compression, and dual exhausts. The 340-hp unit sported solid lifters, plus a larger carb, intake valves, and exhaust manifold. Three-speed manual remained the standard transmission, and Powerglide was again optional; both came with 3.36:1 rear-axle ratios. The extra-cost four-speed manual—which accounted for nearly 82 percent of '63 orders—pulled a standard 3.70 axle but could be ordered with cogs ranging from a lazy 3.08 to a frantic 4.56. Close-ratio internal gearing was provided with the top two engine options.

This page: **The mid-engine Corvette GS-IIb was designed by Larry Shinoda and was reminiscent of his earlier design ideas for the Corvair SS and Monza prototypes. The original GS, the II, was built on a steel chassis. The IIb rode on alloy, hence the "second generation" name.** *Opposite:* **The driver in this promotional photo resembles Corvette engineer Zora Arkus-Duntov—perhaps intentionally. Duntov had tremendous influence on the development of the highly competent Sting Ray—but had no use at all for the gorgeous but impractical split window. Bill Mitchell prevailed in that argument, but only for one season. Come 1964 and the split was gone.**

Only a man with a heart of stone could withstand temptation like this!

You can wear a blindfold, tie yourself to the old family sedan, anything of the kind; but Mister, if you ever hankered to buy a sports car, you're about to become the owner of a new Corvette Sting Ray. Sensible talk about the budget, the good years left in your present car, any kind of rational thought, forget it! Here's why: The new Corvette Sting Ray, available in a sport coupe or a convertible, takes all the excellent characteristics of earlier Corvettes and multiplies them by two. The previous Corvette was the world's most exciting sports car for the last five years, and this new one shows every indication of keeping the title. It has fully independent rear suspension, bigger, self-adjusting brakes, retractable headlights, a V8 engine that's prettier than most girls, and a comprehensive list of extra-cost options like a four-speed transmission, power brakes, monstrous finned brake drums with metallic linings, and Fuel Injection for 360 horsepower. Combine all this with a seating position and a seat-of-the-pants driving sensation like nothing you ever felt, and you've got a car that absolutely will not be denied. And if you're interested enough to have read all this, you might as well stop by the bank on your way to the Chevrolet dealer's. It's fate, man. . . . Chevrolet Division of General Motors, Detroit 2, Michigan.

New CORVETTE STING RAY by Chevrolet

Though the industry's self-imposed 1957 "racing ban" remained in force and General Motors still officially adhered to it, Duntov was determined that anyone who wanted to race a Sting Ray should have the best possible chance of winning. The result was a new track-oriented package, RPO (Regular Production Option) Z06. Priced at a formidable $1818 and limited to fuelie coupes with four-speed and Positraction limited-slip differential, it included finned-aluminum brakes with sintered-metallic linings, heavy-duty front stabilizer bar, uprated shocks, much stiffer springs, and a long-distance 36.5-gallon fuel tank. Also included were handsome new cast-aluminum wheels with genuine knock-off hubs, but they were quickly withdrawn because of a manufacturing flaw that made them too porous to hold air with tubeless tires. Though factory installations are doubtful in '63 production, the multi-spoke rims were soon made right for over-the-counter sale at Chevy dealers.

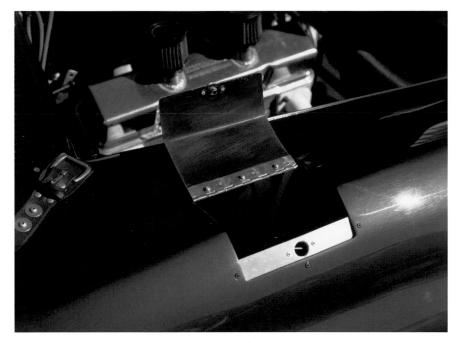

Both pages: Because Ford and Chrysler began to defy the AMA's 1957 racing ban in 1961, GM came in the back door as well, with the Corvette Grand Sport. Built only to race, the Grand Sport was birthed, in part, by Zora Arkus-Duntov, who wanted a credible competitor to Carroll Shelby's Ford-powered AC Cobra. Output from a 327-cid V-8 rebored to 377 was 550 horsepower at 6500 rpm. In pre-competition runs, the Grand Sport's brakes retained too much heat; otherwise, the car tested well. The instrument panel (not shown) was stock Sting Ray but was highlighted by a special 200-mph speedometer. The gauge and control package (left) was businesslike and thorough. One hundred Grand Sports were to be built for homologation purposes, but in January 1963 an internal GM memo made very clear that *sub rosa* racing programs were forbidden. And with that, the Grand Sport was dead.

C2 styling owed much to the Stingray racer, its lines adapted for production by young designer Larry Shinoda under Mitchell's watchful eye. Because of work on the stillborn Q-model, the coupe was developed first, then the convertible. A stretched 2+2 coupe was considered, progressing as far as a full-size mockup, but was rejected as being out of character for Corvette.

Sting Ray prototypes received intensive wind-tunnel testing that resulted in frontal area being trimmed by a square foot, but the sexy shape was prone to undesirable high-speed lift, forcing many racers to apply various aerodynamic aids. On the plus side, the Sting Ray cabin was no less roomy than that of previous Corvettes despite the shorter wheelbase.

The convertible retained Corvette's traditional fold-down cloth roof, solid lift-up top cover, and optional bolt-on hardtop. But all eyes

Both pages: One perk that came with having been a major GM executive was that you were sometimes handed special cars that were one-off variations of established models. Former corporate design chief Harley Earl liked the Sting Ray and was surprised by this unique version, put together by his successor, Bill Mitchell. The leather-lined cockpit had extra gauges, and there was a hopped-up 327 V-8 with dual side exhausts. A 1963 show car had a similar exhaust setup. Special paint and a wide rally stripe brought added panache. The lift-off hardtop was stock.

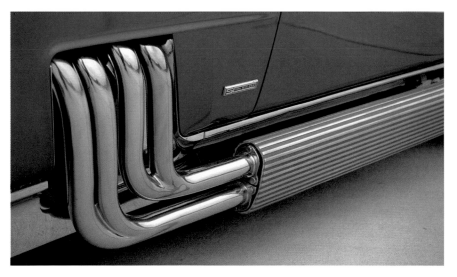

were on the new "split-window" fastback coupe, so-called because its large wrapover backlight was divided by a body-color vertical bar. Duntov lobbied against the "backbone," saying it hampered outward vision. Mitchell huffed in reply that "if you take that off, you might as well forget the whole thing." Duntov prevailed, and a one-piece backlight was substituted after '63, leaving the split-window coupe a one-year model—and more highly prized because of it.

Coupe or convertible, the '63 Sting Rays featured hidden headlights in rotating pods that fit flush with the pointy nose when the lamps were off; humped front and rear fenders; slim L-shape half-bumpers at each end; a revised version of Corvette's now-familiar "ducktail"; and a full-perimeter "character line" at midbody height. Inside was a new "dual cowl" dashboard with a vertical center control panel that dropped down to a floor console, a full set of large gauges, and Corvette's first proper glovebox. Doors cut

into the roof eased entry/exit in the low-slung coupe, but neither body style had a trunklid, doubtless for styling reasons. Cargo had to be stuffed in behind the seats, one of the few things people found to gripe about.

Unsurprisingly, the Sting Ray earned rave reviews from nearly every critic for its handling, grip, and acceleration—not to mention head-turning looks. It won *Car Life* magazine's annual Award for Engineering Excellence, beating out 1963's other big newsmakers, the Buick Riviera and Studebaker Avanti. Straightline performance was as stirring as ever. One published test showed that even a mild 300-hp example with four-speed could do 0–60 mph in 6.1 seconds and the standing quarter-mile in 14.5 at 100 mph. *Motor Trend*'s four-speed fuelie coupe with 3.70 axle ran 5.8 seconds and 14.5 at 102 mph. *MT*'s tester also returned better than 18 miles per gallon at legal highway speeds and 14.1 mpg overall.

Both pages: Today, the 1963 Sting Ray is the ultimate dream car of countless enthusiasts, many of whom were not even born when this striking car was new. As a reflection of increasing buyer interest in more civilized sports cars, options expanded this year. Power brakes went into 15 percent of '63 production, power steering into 12 percent. But only 278 buyers went for the $421 air conditioning; and leather upholstery, which could be had for just $81, was installed in only about 400 cars, from a production total of some 21,600. On the other hand, more than 18,000 Sting Rays—better than four of every five—came with the four-speed manual transmission.

With its great all-around ability and arresting appearance, the Sting Ray quickly proved the most popular 'Vette yet. In fact, sales in the first model year were nearly twice the record '62 total at 21,513 (10,594 coupes, 10,919 ragtops). Performance had less to do with this than the wider market appeal of new extra-cost creature comforts: leather upholstery, power steering, power brakes (at last), AM/FM radio, air conditioning, and more.

The Sting Ray would see a number of worthwhile improvements over the next four years. The '64s, for example, gained more-durable shock absorbers and swapped constant-rate front coil springs for more-efficient variable-rate units. Further enhancing ride and refinement were added sound insulation, revised body and transmission mounts, and extra bushings to quiet the shift linkage. The 250- and 300-hp V-8s stood pat, but the solid-lifter 350-hp unit got a high-lift cam and a new Holley carburetor

Opposite, top, and this page: The unique "split" rear window went away for 1964, improving visibility but robbing the Sting Ray of a bit of its personality. In a move that some would later regret, many splits were converted by their owners to single pieces. Thankfully, the fake hood vents were abandoned for 1964. Instrumentation was clear and nicely grouped in front of drivers. *Opposite, bottom:* More views of the ferocious, but doomed, Grand Sport racer.

(replacing a four-barrel Carter) to produce 365 hp. The "fuelie" also gained 15 horses, reaching 375, but its price went up to $538. Four-speed manual transmission still cost $188 but was now GM's own "Muncie" gearbox instead of a Borg-Warner. The expected minor trim changes occurred, most notably removal of the dummy hood vents. Coupes sported the aforementioned one-piece rear window, and their decorative air-exhaust vent on the left-rear roof pillar was made functional. Helped by unchanged base prices—$4037 for the convertible, $4252 for the coupe—sales set another record at 22,229. Coupe volume dropped to 8304 units, but convertible orders more than compensated, rising to 13,925.

Both pages: Chevy produced 13,925 convertible roadsters for 1964; at 8304, the year's coupes didn't come close. Available engines, each of them a 327-cid V-8, came in three flavors: 250, 300/365, and 360 horsepower. The last was fuel injected. All three iterations shared a 4.00 × 3.25 bore × stroke. Inside, the twin-cowl dash and instrument panel offered the full complement of gauges that sports car buyers now insisted upon. The cars' four-speed manual gearboxes were made at GM's Muncie, Indiana, plant.

Both pages: Coupe production for 1965 was 8186, holding at about the 1964 level. All 'Vettes lost their hood indentations for '65. Four-wheel disc brakes now were optional; likewise a big-block V-8, the 396-cid, 425-hp Mark IV/Turbo Jet V-8. The 327 with 300 horses remained a popular option.

The total was 23,652 for 1965, when the hood's vent scallops were filled in and front fenders sprouted three working exhaust vents instead of nonfunctional "speedlines." But the big news was the arrival of standard four-wheel disc brakes. A four-piston design with two-piece calipers and rotor cooling fins, the new binders had much greater swept area than the previous drums (still available as a credit option) and markedly stronger stopping power. Even better, they were virtually fade-free in repeated hard use and, of course, were unaffected by wet weather.

Speed freaks applauded the mid-1965 debut of Corvette's first big-block V-8 option. Officially called Mark IV and marketed as the "Turbo Jet,"

continued on page 62

Both pages: Bill Mitchell (shown) named his predictive Mako II concept after the mako shark, which fascinated him. Mitchell told Consumer Guide®, "We used a dark top and light underbody, and nobody had ever done that . . . . It's even got nice lines from the top." The Mako ran with a 650-horse Can Am competition engine.

it was derived from a stillborn 1963 NASCAR racing engine and was notable for an unusually complex valvetrain. It arrived with 396 cubic inches and, for Corvettes, a nominal 425 hp via a big four-barrel carburetor, solid lifters, and tight 11.0:1 compression. Performance was predictably sizzling, with quarter-mile sprints of around 14 seconds at 102–104 mph. Sensibly, Chevy threw in stiffer suspension, super-duty clutch, and larger radiator and fan, plus side exhaust pipes and a domed hood, yet charged less than $300 for the lot. Small-block choices were basically as before, but the base 327 gained 50 hp to reach 300 and the step-up option did likewise to hit 350.

Both pages: This '65 convertible (wearing its removable hardtop) came off the line with the Mark IV/Turbo Jet 396. The engine was called the "Porcupine" because of pushrods tilted at odd angles—one result of working backward by designing the ports and manifolds first, rather than starting with the combustion chambers. After the basic head configuration was tested for optimal breathing, it was frozen and all other components subsequently designed around it. Like the head, the Mark IV block was all new. With hydraulic lifters, a four-barrel carburetor, and 11.0:1 compression, the motor came to Corvette with 425 horsepower. Thus equipped, the car ran the quarter in about 14 seconds at 102–104 mph. Top speed was 140, though 160 mph was possible with axle ratios lower than 3.70:1.

For 1966, Chevy responded to the Ford-powered 427 Shelby Cobras that were eating Corvette's lunch on both road and track. The result was a Mark IV bored out to—you guessed it—427 cubes. It was offered with 390 hp on 10.25:1 compression and 425 hp with an 11:1 squeeze. While the latter had the same horse count as the 396, it packed usefully more torque—460 pound-feet versus 415. Though the 427 was sold only with Positraction and the close-ratio four-speed as "mandatory options," Chevy again included a fortified suspension and cooling system, plus stouter rear halfshafts and U-joints. Performance bordered on the incredible. A 425-hp car with the short 4.11:1 axle clocked 0–60 mph in just 4.8 seconds and 0–100 mph in 11.2 on the way to 140 mph maximum. Acceleration was hardly less impressive with more-modest 3.36 gearing, *Car and Driver* reporting 0–60 in 5.4 seconds and a standing quarter of 12.8 at 112 mph.

With muscle cars now all the rage, Chevy dropped the fuelie 327 due to high costs and low demand. It also dropped the two top-power carbureted small-blocks, leaving the 300- and 350-hp versions and their associated transmissions. Otherwise, 1966 was a quiet Corvette year: an eggcrate grille insert to replace horizontal bars, unadorned rear roof pillars for coupes, and more minor-trim and equipment shuffles. Even so, sales set yet another record, rising to 27,720, with convertibles again way outpolling coupes.

A redesigned Corvette was planned for 1967 but fell behind schedule, so the Sting Ray hung on for one more year. Prices had risen lately, but not much; the convertible now started at $4241, the coupe at $4389. Spotter's points were limited to five smaller front-fender vents, unadorned rocker panels, a single oblong central backup lamp, and,

Both pages: Corvette styling was altered very little for 1966 and largely stood pat for '67 (shown). One change was a one-year-only solo backup light, situated above the license plate. The knock-off wheel hubs were deleted and replaced with slotted six-inch Rally wheels with chrome beauty rings and concealed lug nuts. Inside, the handbrake moved from beneath the dash to between the seats. The two small-block V-8s returned, but the big 427s switched to triple two-barrel carbs, elevating horsepower by ten, to 400 and a stated 435 (though true output was higher).

replacing standard wheel covers, slotted Rally wheels with chrome "beauty rings" and hub centers. The main interior revision was moving the parking-brake handle from below the dash to between the seats.

The headline engine news was switching the top two big-block V-8s to triple two-barrel carburetors, resulting in an extra 10 horses for new ratings of 400 and 435. The latter, RPO L71, again featured 11.1 compression, solid lifters, and transistorized ignition. There was also an L89 version with aluminum cylinder heads (versus cast iron), larger exhaust valves—and the same grossly understated horsepower. Wildest of all was the new L88, a virtual racing engine. This was basically the L89 with an even hotter cam, stratospheric 12.5:1 compression, a huge four-barrel Holley, small-diameter flywheel, and aluminum radiator. Though nominal horsepower was 430, actual output was around 560. But the L88 option cost a staggering $1500, required several mandatory extras, needed 103-octane racing fuel, and wasn't available with radio and heater. No wonder only 20 such '67 'Vettes were built. Total sales eased to 22,940, as the coming '68 redesign was an open secret and some buyers decided to wait a year.

Though racing Sting Rays often bowed to Ferraris and Shelby Cobras, privateers gave Chevrolet publicists a good many victories to trumpet. For example, Don Yenko was SCCA national B-Production champ in 1963, a Roger Penske car won its class at Nassau '65, and 1966 saw Sting Rays place 12th overall in the Daytona Continental and ninth at Sebring.

The Sting Ray might have been a world-beating racer had Zora Arkus-Duntov been given a free hand. In mid-1962, the Corvette's proud chief engineer set to work on a lightweight racing version of the forthcoming Sting Ray coupe. The aim was to win the 1963 World Manufacturer's Championship road-racing series, where grand-touring cars like Corvette and Cobra were newly eligible. Though heartily endorsed by Chevy chief Bunkie Knudsen, the project was super-secret, as it defied both General Motors policy and the industry's still-prevailing "no-racing"

Both pages: Corvette's second generation made its competition debut at the 24 Hours of Le Mans in 1967, in a car driven by Dick Guldstrand and Bob Bondurant. The Corvette was sponsored by Dana Chevrolet, a dealership located in Southern California. The L-88 engine was an aluminum-head 427 tweaked to develop about 600 horsepower. Guldstrand took the Le Mans 'Vette to a shade over 170 mph on the Mulsanne straight (a new record), but the engine was overmatched by the demands of the race and gave out at around the halfway mark. No other Corvette of the Sting Ray generation competed at Le Mans.

Sunoco 260 Powers Corvette to G.T. Championship at Sebring

Sunoco 260, the same fuel you can buy in any Sunoco station, powered Roger Penske's Sting Ray to victory in the Grand Touring Class at Sebring. The Penske car averaged 87.1 miles per hour during the 12-hour race.

In addition to pump-grade Sunoco 260 in the tank, the Corvette Sting Ray was completely lubricated throughout the race with Sunoco Products.

Stop at Sunoco . . . go with confidence!

MOTOR TREND / JUNE 1966 15

edict. The result, called Grand Sport, employed every speed and handling trick Duntov could muster: racing-style suspension and tubular-steel inner structure, aerodynamic tweaks, and a unique hemi-head, 377-cid small-block V-8 good for at least 550 hp. With all that and more, the 2000-pound GS promised to be a very serious competitor.

Then top GM managers learned of what was going on and summarily canceled the project in January 1963, at which point only five Grand Sports had been built out of a planned 100. But Duntov was determined and saw to it that the cars were sold to well-heeled racers who could realize the

Grand Sport's potential. Alas, the GS would score no major wins, even though the five cars changed hands several times through 1966. (Two were converted into roadsters for races requiring that configuration.) The car's best showing came at Nassau in December 1963, with high overall finishes and class victories in two events. Happily, all five Grand Sports survive as reminders of what might have been.

Brief though it was, the Sting Ray era took Chevrolet's sports car to much higher levels of sophistication, excitement, and popularity. It would be a tough act to follow.

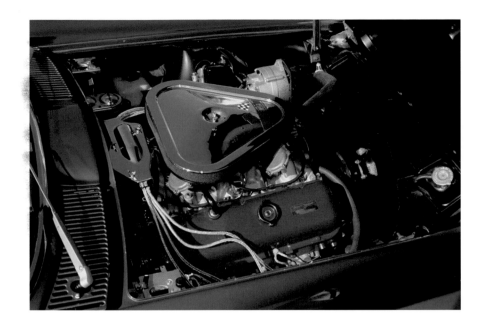

Both pages: Chevy had slated the '66 Corvette as the last of the Sting Ray generation, but because of developmental problems with the follow-on, the Sting Ray stayed around for 1967—and became the most sophisticated and polished car of generation two. Chevy's 3 × 2 427 (shown) developed 390/435 horsepower this year and was simultaneously powerful and tractable. But the race-bred L-88 427 was also available to the public, mainly for sanctioned racing. Heater and radio were deleted from L-88 cars to discourage street use, and buyers took Positraction, H-D suspension, and other competition tweaks as "mandatory options." Gulping 103-octane fuel exclusively, the L-88 gave a rough idle and wasn't easy to start (the ignition was transistorized). The L-88 also cost an extra $1500, a great deal of money in the mid-Sixties—so great, in fact, that only 20 L-88 Corvettes were ordered and produced.

3

Longest-lived of all Corvettes, the shovel-nosed "Shark" flourished for an astounding 15 seasons, even as power waned. Though controversial to some, the Shark struck just the right note with many.

1968–1982: OH, THE SHARK, BABE, HAS SUCH TEETH, DEAR

It wasn't the Corvette many had hoped for, nor what some at General Motors had wanted. Yet the "C3" or "Shark" would last 15 model years, by far the longest run of any Corvette generation before or since (so far). Such staying power is rare in the car business, but the C3 is even more remarkable for surviving through an era of new federal safety, emissions, and fuel-economy mandates; soaring gas prices and insurance rates that devastated the performance-car market; two unprecedented energy crises; and increasing import-brand competition.

During the course of its run, the Shark improved build quality and ergonomics, even as federal mandates sucked away much of the horsepower. Throughout much of the Seventies, Corvette was miles removed from its days of previous peak performance, but the car's mystique held fast. Sales soared as Chevy successfully recast the 'Vette as a stylish *boulevardier*.

Initial work on the Shark began in early 1964 and was influenced by the advent of racing-inspired mid-engine road cars, where powerplants sit behind the cockpit, ahead of the rear axleline, and drive the aft wheels through a combined transmission/differential or transaxle. Corvette chief engineer Zora Duntov had explored this configuration with the 1960 CERV I (Chevrolet Experimental Racing Vehicle), an open-wheel single-seater. Based on that and subsequent work by GM engineers, the C3 was first envisioned as a "midships" design, with proposals submitted by a Chevrolet Engineering team under Frank Winchell, a group headed by Duntov, and Bill Mitchell's crew at GM Design Staff.

Trouble was, GM had yet to devise a transaxle that could reliably cope with the torque of a high-power engine, and the cost of engineering and tooling a midships powertrain for one relatively low-volume model would have sent Corvette prices to the moon. But there was no need for it anyway. Sure, many enthusiasts might have *liked* an American reply to mid-engine European exotics like the Lamborghini Miura, but whether they'd actually buy one was open to question. Besides, consistently strong Sting Ray sales suggested that most 'Vette buyers were quite happy with the traditional front-engine layout.

Ultimately, cost, feasibility, and time constraints dictated that the

Opposite: Model-year 1968 ushered in the "Shark" generation, or C3 Corvette, with styling inspired by Bill Mitchell's 1965 Mako Shark II dream car. That concept was recycled, with alterations, for the 1969 auto-show season as the Manta Ray, shown here. *This page:* Mitchell poses with the Mako II and a production '68 in a GM publicity photo. His staff worked overtime to get the show car's blue-to-silver paint job to resemble an actual shark.

C3 would amount to a new body on the still-competitive Sting Ray chassis. And what a body: adapted from Mitchell's slinky, muscular 1965 Mako Shark II show car—hence the Shark nickname—by Henry Haga of Chevrolet Styling, then headed by David Holls.

The C3 arrived for 1968, the first year for federally mandated safety equipment and exhaust-emission controls. The Sting Ray name was banished, but coupe and convertible body styles returned. The latter retained its soft top, hinged top cover, and optional hardtop, but the coupe was a new notchback design with an innovative "T-top" roof: twin panels that could be lifted-off to create a semi-convertible. The coupe also sported "flying buttress" roof pillars flanking a removable upright rear window, a treatment stylists called the "sugar scoop." Both body styles featured a low, pointed nose with flip-up headlamps; fulsome fenders housing 7-inch-wide wheels for added cornering grip; and a neatly cropped tail with four round lights and a tiny spoiler. Door vent windows

Both pages: **Though the '68 retained Corvette's customary long-hood/short-deck proportions and the Sting Ray's curved fenderlines and four-taillamp motif, the look was far more muscular. Aerodynamics figured in a newly cropped tail topped by a small lip spoiler—but again with no trunklid. The rear roof was Ferrari-inspired, with "flying buttress" sail panels astride a newly upright and removable rear window. Also for aero reasons, the '68 was a "bottom breather," the engine taking in air from beneath the nose; the grille was mostly decorative. Susie and Bobby dig it.**

You pull up to a traffic light. Heads turn. You look in the rearview mirror. Eyes follow. Corvette's that kind of car. The kind of car that makes you feel the whole world is watching. The kind of car that brings out the driver in you. And why not? Everything's in your favor. Sleek aerodynamic fuselage. Four-wheel disc brakes. Independent suspension all around. Even V8s available up to 427 cubic inches. That's the real beauty **Corvette** *CHEVROLET* of Corvette. It does all the work, you get all the credit.

Superiority complex.

Corvette Sting Ray Convertible. Sports Class winner of Motor Trend's 1968 Achievement Award

'68 Corvettes fitted with the 427-cid V-8 developed 390 or 435 horsepower—plenty o' power no matter how you look at it. Bore × stroke was 4.25 × 3.76. Flush door handles and flying-buttress-style backlight treatment were cool, but the car still had no opening trunklid.

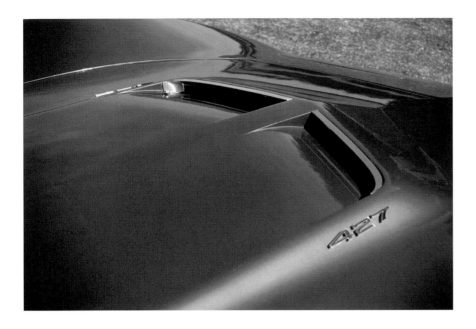

were eliminated with adoption of Chevrolet's new flow-through "Astro Ventilation." An opening trunklid remained conspicuously absent, however.

Wheelbase held at 98 inches, but overall length stretched to 182.1 inches, up seven from the Sting Ray. Overall height dropped by two inches to 47.8, and overall width slimmed by 0.4 inch. Curb weights changed little, the ragtop gaining 65 pounds (to 3425), the coupe losing 100 (to 3260).

The engine lineup was basically a '67 rerun, with 300- and 350-horsepower 327 small-blocks and big-block 427s with hp ratings of 390, 400, 430, and 435. Three- and four-speed manual transmissions also returned, but the archaic Powerglide automatic option was finally replaced by GM's modern three-speed Turbo Hydra-Matic. Another plus was moving the battery from beneath the hood to behind the seats for better weight distribution.

The C3 would have bowed for 1967 had Duntov not delayed it to address excessive high-speed front-end lift, inadequate engine cooling, and poor rigidity with the original one-piece liftoff roof panel. The first two problems were alleviated by aero-functional front-fender vents and a small "chin" spoiler; the last was solved with a longitudinal spar between the windshield header and rear roof section, resulting in the T-bar roof.

But plenty of problems remained. The most glaring was poor workmanship that led one journalist to label his Corvette loaner "unfit to road test." Other writers judged the new design needlessly gimmicky. The wipers, for example, now lurked beneath a pop-up vacuum-operated cowl panel that didn't always pop in frosty weather. A narrower cockpit (a penalty of the wasp-waisted styling), less luggage space, no glovebox, and poor interior airflow won no friends. Neither did still-inadequate cooling on big-block cars and a much harder ride even with the standard suspension. Yet despite all that, the '68 set another Corvette sales record at more than 28,500 units. Convertibles again outpolled coupes, this year by nearly two to one. One likely reason is that the coupe's base price jumped nearly $300 to $4663, while the ragtop went up less than $100, to $4320.

Both pages: Like some other '68 Chevrolets, the new Shark Corvette eliminated door vent windows by adopting the brand's new flow-through "Astro Ventilation" that ducted air from the cowl to dashboard outlets and out through vents at the rear. Four front-fender gills recalled the '67 Sting Ray and were also functional. A removable hard top remained an option for ragtops like this one. The convertible again outsold the Corvette coupe for '68, but this would be the last time it would do so.

Total sales soared to 38,762 for '69, when coupes outsold convertibles (despite modest price hikes for both) and the Stingray name returned—as one word—in front-fender script. Duntov kept working on inherent flaws, finding a little more cockpit space (smaller steering wheel, thinner door panels), adding an override switch for the wiper cover, and reworking other bits. Detail styling changes involved neater outside door handles, black instead of chrome grille bars, and backup lights integrated with the inboard taillights. Cornering grip improved via standard 8-inch-wide wheels, and the frame was stiffened. A locking steering-column ignition switch replaced the previous in-dash device, per federal decree, and the instrument panel tacked on a map pocket.

Besides lower compression ratios for all '69 engines, emissions considerations prompted stroking the small-block V-8 to 350 cubic inches, though power ratings were still 300 and 350. A fourth 427 option appeared with a nominal 430 hp and available axle ratios ranging from 4.56:1 to 2.75:1. Even wilder was the all-aluminum ZL1 big-block, a genuine Can-Am racing engine priced at a formidable $4718. Production? Just two.

Speaking of racing, Corvette reasserted itself in SCCA competition, as the Shelby Cobras had retired. Chevy engineer Jerry Thompson and driver Tony DeLorenzo teamed up to take the '69 A-Production national championship, while Allan Barker claimed the B-Production crown and would do so for the next three seasons. Corvette also celebrated a production milestone in 1969 as number 250,000 came off the St. Louis line—and this from a car that had been near death barely 15 years earlier.

Both pages: After a year as just "Corvette," Chevrolet's sports car was a Stingray once again for 1969, but with the name spelled as one word on the front fenders. This 427 coupe shows off the side exhaust pipes that remained a fairly popular option for big-block 'Vettes, plus the new-for-'69 blackout grille and integrated backup lamps. Dashboards added map pockets, but engines, big-blocks included, subtracted some power for the sake of cleaner air. This model year also saw production of the quarter-millionth Corvette since 1953.

A two-month autoworkers' strike slashed 1970 volume by some 50 percent to 17,316 units, the lowest model-year total in eight years. The main news that season was a big-block punched out to 454 cid, again to meet emissions standards that were increasingly sapping power from all Detroit engines. Even so, lower compression left the LS5 version with "only" 390 hp. A more-powerful LS7 rated at 460 hp was advertised and a few prototype installations were tried, but the option was never offered for sale because it couldn't be made "clean" enough.

The rest of the car was again little changed—a fine-check grille and front-fender vents provided visual ID—but Chevrolet cleaned up more details and belatedly offered a 370-hp solid-lifter small-block that had been promised for '69. Designated LT-1, sold only with four-speed manual and sitting beneath a bulged hood, it offered near big-block performance, with typical quarter-mile runs of 14.2 seconds at 102 mph. Back at the track, Corvette repeated as SCCA A-Production champ in 1970, with a young John Greenwood taking the honors. He did so again the following year, then teamed up with comedian Dick Smothers to place first in the GT class at Sebring in 1972.

Opposite, *far left:* GM worked on more ideas for a possible mid-engine Corvette with the 1970 XP-882 experimental and a later rebodied version with gullwing doors and a prototype Wankel rotary engine. *Other photos:* A fine-check grille and side vents identified 1970 Corvettes, as did square exhaust ports. A big-block V-8 enlarged to 454 cubes was among the few noteworthy changes in a year when production plunged by half, due to an autoworkers' strike.

Sales recovered a bit for 1971, rising to 21,801. Still-lower compression (to accommodate low-lead gas) dropped the base small-block to 270 hp, the LT1 to 330, the big LS5 to 365. The aborted aluminum-head LS7 returned as an emissions-friendly all-iron LS6 putting out 425 hp. Reflecting period inflation, base prices were up to $5259 for the ragtop and $5496 for the coupe.

Further detuning occurred for '72, when a switch to more-realistic SAE net power ratings made engines seem even punier. The LS6 was canceled, a sign of the times, while the LS5 returned with 270 net hp. Small-blocks were down to base and LT1 with a respective 200- and 255-hp net. There were few other changes. The fiber-optic exterior light monitors available since '68 were dropped, the center console was redesigned, and the once-optional antitheft alarm system became standard, a nod to the 'Vette's high "thievability." For all the discouraging news, sales went up again, reaching 26,994.

Both pages: This 1972 convertible carries the solid-lifter LT1 V-8 introduced in 1970 as the most potent 350 small-block available. But 1971 detuning for low-lead fuel sapped power, taking 40 hp from the LT1 and leaving it with 330. In 1971, as before, a special domed hood and badging were included with the LT1 option. Whitewall tires were starting to fade from public favor, but could still nicely dress up a 'Vette.

The '73s gained a body-color nose of pliable plastic—the Shark's first major styling change—that met the government's new "5-mph bumper" rule, added two inches to overall length, and looked terrific. More sound insulation and new chassis mounts made all 'Vettes a bit quieter. The coupe's rear window was now fixed, and the LT1 small-block went away. Rear-impact standards dictated a matching body-color tail for the '74s (upping overall length to 185.1 inches), which arrived with the Middle East oil embargo, still-higher gas prices, and long lines at the pumps. Engines were down to base L48 and step-up L82 small-blocks, with each losing five hp, and a lone 270-hp LS4 big-block. Prices kept rising—the '74 coupe broke $6000—but so did model-year sales, which

Opposite, bottom left: Though based on Chevy's subcompact Vega, the plastic-bodied 1973 XP-898 exercise hints at the future C4 Corvette and 1982 Camaro ponycar. *Bottom right:* Shown in 1973, the small, mid-engine XP-897 GT was designed around a proposed Wankel rotary that never materialized. *Other photos:* The Shark's first major styling change, a new federally mandated "soft" nose, arrived for 1973.

hit 30,464 for '73, then 37,502. The reason, of course, is that there was still nothing else like the Corvette on the market, even if the car had become a lot tamer.

Underscoring that point, 'Vette performance was further downgraded for 1975. The big-block engine was canceled, and small-block hp dropped to 165 for the L48 and 205 for the L82 despite adoption of catalytic converters (for lower emissions) and more-reliable electronic ignition. Visual changes were confined to pairs of small black bumper pads and eliminating the faux rear-deck air-extractor vents. Despite the continuing sameness, sales went up to 38,465.

Opposite, top right: Still toying with mid-engine ideas in 1972, GM put newly styled bodies on its two XP-882 chassis. One body was made entirely of aluminum in cooperation with Reynolds Metals Co. *Other photos:* A nose-matching "soft" body-color rear end marked 1974 Corvettes. Engines were reduced to a pair of small-blocks and a final 454.

But convertible sales had been waning since 1968, so the ragtop was dropped for '76. (It would return 10 years later.) Horsepower went up for a change, to 180/210, thanks to a freer-breathing intake system. The price of admission was now $7605 minimum, yet sales rose again, reaching 46,558.

The Stingray name disappeared again for '77, when base price jumped to $8648, in part because power steering, power brakes, and leather upholstery were made standard. Interiors were updated with new gauge graphics, a reworked center console, and a shorter steering column mounting a new "Smart Switch" stalk controlling wiper/washer and headlamp dimmer. The Shark was now a decade old, yet sales set another record: an improbable 49,213.

This page: In profile, the '75 convertible highlighted how well the "5-mph" front and rear ends were integrated with the original Shark styling. *Opposite:* The 1975 Corvette Mulsanne concept put bright metallic silver paint atop 1975 styling cues, though the domed hood (bracketed by recessed, functional vents) and inset, rectangular headlamps were strictly conceptual. The Mulsanne ran with a ZL1 engine bored out to 454 cubic inches and fitted with an in-development Rochester fuel injection system.

GM had been teasing enthusiasts since the late 1960s with a procession of concepts that hinted a mid-engine Corvette was just around the corner. It wasn't, of course, but it did come close. Its basis would have been the Aerovette, the renamed V-8-powered iteration of the 1972 Wankel-engine "Four Rotor" concept. Nagged by Bill Mitchell, GM president Tom Murphy actually approved a productionized Aerovette for 1980. Then Mitchell retired in 1977, and the program was soon abandoned. Zora Duntov, another booster, had retired at the end of '74, and his successor as Corvette chief engineer, David R. McLellan, espoused the "front mid-engine" format for reasons of packaging, manufacturing, performance, and cost. By mid-1978, McLellan and company were working on a conventional but all-new C4.

Opposite and this page, right: Small black bumper guards were the 'Vette's only new visual for '75. The ragtop Shark was in its final year, due to steadily declining sales. This car's luggage rack and steering-wheel cover are non-stock accessories. *Above:* "...in an age of reality." The reality was that performance-car performance was drying up. The year's top 350 V-8 put out just 205 horsepower.

To fill the gap, the Shark was spruced up for Corvette's 25th birthday year, gaining a Sting Ray-style fastback roofline with compound-curve rear window. The '78 also received a host of minor changes: first-time-available 60-series tires, a larger fuel tank, redesigned gauges and wiper switch, a roller-blind shade for the now-exposed cargo area, Silver Anniversary badges, optional two-toning (the first since '61), and available glass T-tops (delayed from '77). Corvette was chosen pace car for that year's Indy 500, and Chevrolet issued 6502 Limited Edition Indy Pace Car Replicas with special paint, leather interior, unique lightweight seats, and owner-applied

Both pages: A mid-engine Corvette was close to production for 1980 until GM decided to opt for a fresh front-engine design. To fill the gap, the faithful Shark was given a fastback roof and other cosmetic updates for '78—plus commemorative badges for the car's Silver Anniversary year. Engines were down to a pair of small-block V-8s that included a newly optional 220-hp L82.

pace-car decals. It sold for $13,653, a big jump from the $9351 standard model. Which explains why, to the division's chagrin, fast-buck artists were quick to convert standard 'Vettes into bogus replicas, creating no little confusion. There was also a Silver Anniversary '78, actually a trim package and not that different from stock.

Engine choices were down to two 350s: standard 185-hp L48 and extra-cost 220-hp L82. Road tests showed the latter could deliver 0–60 mph in 6.5 seconds and a 15.2-second quarter-mile at 95 mph—tepid by late-'60s standards, but pretty good for 1978. So were Corvette sales, though the total slipped to 46,776, including Pace Car Replicas.

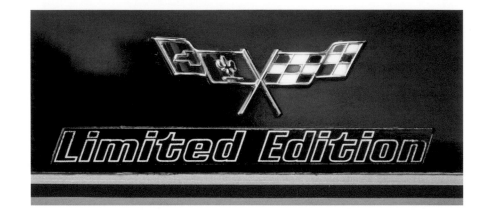

Both pages: Corvette paced another Indy 500 in 1978, and 6502 Limited Edition Indy Pace Car Replicas were built to celebrate. To Chevy's chagrin, the stiff $13,653 price prompted numerous knock-offs by quick-buck artists, creating a PR nightmare.

The '79 tally, however, was 53,807, another record. Changes were modest: new seats and optional front and rear spoilers borrowed from the Pace Car, standard halogen high-beam headlamps, and minor trim changes. Pricing also set a record at $10,220 minimum.

Corvette went on a diet for 1980, losing some 150 pounds via wider use of plastics and by substituting aluminum for steel in the differential housing and front frame crossmember. Aerodynamics improved via a new sloped nose with integral spoiler, plus a faired-in rear spoiler. These measures were timely, as another gas crunch occurred in early 1979 and even performance buyers were thinking mpg as much as mph. Air conditioning and tilt/telescope steering wheel shifted from optional to standard status, and the speedometer now read to only 85 mph, per a new mileage-minded federal mandate. Energy Crisis II had triggered a sharp recession that clobbered car sales all over, and the 'Vette was no exception, production dropping to 40,614.

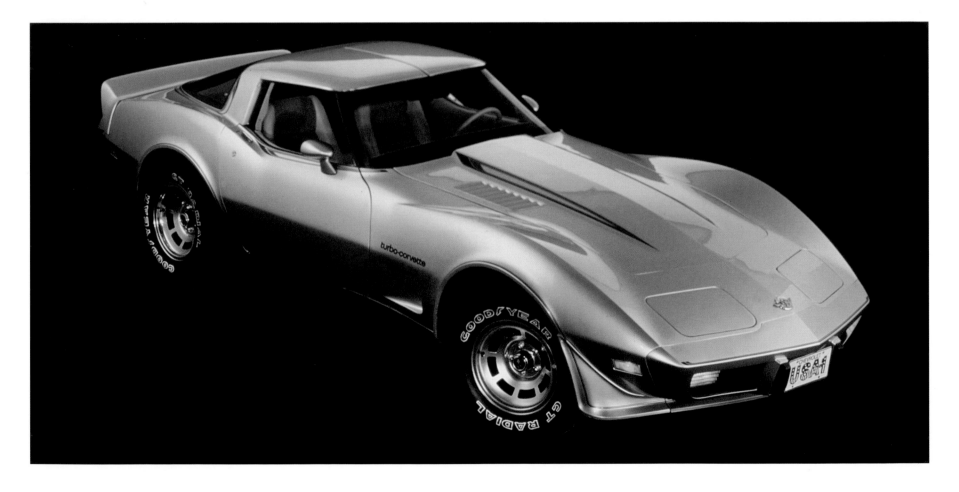

Both pages: Turbocharging was the Next Big Thing on the late-Seventies performance scene, and Chevy dabbled with force-fed concepts that included two production-based examples, and a two-tone called Turbo Vette 3. All used 350 V-8s with exhaust-driven Garrett turbos that were claimed to bump horsepower by up to 30 percent. But Chevy soon abandoned its turbo program and borrowed blown engines from Buick, which was GM's lead division in this area.

Both pages: Corvette emphasized fuel efficiency for performance-starved 1981 by losing 150 pounds, enhancing the aerodynamic front and rear spoilers that had been adopted the previous year.

More weight-saving occurred for '81, mainly from a fiberglass rear leaf spring (replacing steel) and thinner glass for door windows and the optional see-through T-tops. There was now just one 350 V-8, a new 190-hp L81 with magnesium rocker covers, stainless-steel exhaust manifold, and GM's Computer Command Control engine-management system. Government fuel-economy mandates dictated a lockup torque converter for the optional automatic transmission. Inflation pushed base price past $15,000, yet model-year volume held steady at 40,606. This year saw the historic transfer of production from St. Louis to a new high-tech plant in Bowling Green, Kentucky, built exclusively for Corvette. With it came promises of improved workmanship.

The move to Kentucky suggested that a redesigned Corvette was coming at last. It was, but not before the Shark took a final bow. Previewing the next-generation drivetrain, the 1982 edition sported a thoroughly revised L83 engine with 200 hp, thanks to GM's new "Cross-Fire" fuel injection—the first fuelie Corvette since 1965. And for the first time since 1955, there was no manual gearbox, just a new four-speed automatic with torque-converter lockup on all forward gears save first. But the kicker was another limited-production job tellingly named Collector Edition. It was the costliest 'Vette yet at $22,537 but came with many unique features including a lift-up rear window (belatedly), "turbine" alloy wheels (shades of '63), bronze-tint glass T-tops, and a specific silver/beige color scheme. This time, Chevy avoided forgeries by building as many Collectors as customers demanded, which amounted to 6759. Total sales, though, plunged to 25,407, the lowest in a decade.

No matter. The C3 had survived one of the worst periods in U.S. automotive history. And if events forced its personality to change, a tamer Corvette was surely better than none at all. For that reason alone, the Shark will always be one of Motown's greatest hits.

Both pages: The Shark took its final bow for 1982, with a small-block V-8 fitted with standard fuel injection—the first in 17 years—plus a more efficient four-speed automatic transmission. Also new was a tellingly named Collector Edition model with a lift-up hatchback window, a silver/beige paint scheme with "fadeaway" accents, bronze-tint T-tops, and more. It was the costliest 'Vette yet at $22,357, which may be why only 6759 were built. Total Corvette sales for the model year fell to a decade low, and the C3 was past its competitive prime. Chevy was finally about to introduce a new and fully up-to-date version of America's sports car.

Even as Corvette was made smoother, more svelte, and hyper-efficient, sales slipped. Some startling price increases didn't help, but the fourth-generation 'Vette persevered and hung on for 12 seasons.

1984–1990: FASTER, LEANER... AND IN TROUBLE

The much-anticipated C4 bowed in early 1983 as an '84 model, causing some to wonder why General Motors would skip Corvette's milestone 30th birthday year. GM hadn't forgotten. Rather, the car's introduction date had slipped just enough from the original target that engineers found it more expedient to tune for 1984 federal emissions standards.

Few cars have been more eagerly anticipated than the fourth-generation 'Vette (or, to its fans, C4). After 15 seasons of the Shark,

Corvette was about to be recast for the Eighties. Somewhat smaller and leaner, and less obviously shapely, the C4 was a gorgeous wedge that spoke in confidently measured tones where the Shark had tried to shout. The new generation wasn't an anniversary issue, but it pointed Corvette in a fresh, wholly new direction.

Historians may have huffed, but most everyone else was enthusiastic about the fourth-generation 'Vette. Not only had it been a long time coming, it was completely new except for the powertrain, and even that was updated. Still, like the Shark before it, the C4 provoked controversy and arrived with some rough edges. But it was a great advance in Corvette design and engineering, and Chevrolet would make it even better over an admirable 12-year run.

As noted in the previous chapter, the C4 program was underway by mid-1978. It marked the closest collaboration yet among GM designers and engineers, respectively led in this instance by Jerry Palmer, then head of Chevrolet Studio Three, and David R. McLellan, who succeeded Zora Arkus-Duntov as Corvette chief engineer in 1974. Development took note of stronger competition from import-brand sports cars and looming new federal regulations. Key goals included improving both fuel economy and performance via increased powertrain efficiency, wind-cheater styling, and close attention to weight, plus even better handling and greater rigidity, quietness, and cockpit space.

The C4 debuted as a fastback coupe that looked nothing like the Shark but retained now-traditional Corvette hallmarks: pop-up headlamps, a low nose, curvy fenderlines, and a short tail with four round lamps. The overall shape, however, was more "organic" than the C3's, with fuller bodysides that implied extra hip and shoulder room, plus a lower beltline for better visibility. With its smoother contours and more steeply raked windshield, the C4 claimed a 0.34 drag coefficient, unexceptional even then, but a useful 23.7-percent slicker than the C3's 0.44. A lift-up hatch window returned from the '82 Collector Edition, but the old T-tops gave way to a one-piece roof panel, and a new front-hinged "clamshell" hood/fender assembly offered superb engine access. Most people liked this package, though some criticized it as bland. Among them was former GM design chief Bill Mitchell, who likened the C4 to a grouper fish.

Dimensional changes were significant, but not obvious. Wheelbase shrank by nearly 2 inches (to 96), but designers also cut overall length by a whopping 8.8 inches (to 176.5), expanded width by 2 inches (to 71), and lopped 1.3 inches from overall height (to 46.7).

Opposite: The all-new 1984 C4 had been expected for '83, Corvette's 30th birthday year, but development was delayed just enough to make an '84 introduction more practical. *This page, top right:* C4 styling and dimensions were pretty much locked up by late 1979, when this full-size clay model was photographed. *Center and lower right:* These mid-1970s sketches predate the start of C4 development and were likely part of the aborted 1980 midships model based on the XP-822 "Aerovette" concept. *Below:* Many of the great Italian coachbuilder/design firms have let their imaginations roam on Corvette chassis. This exercise from the house of Bertone was called Ramarro and premiered at the 1984 L.A. Auto Expo. Note the ultra-low canopy-style roof and geometric lower-body lines. The car was finished in three shades of green.

As expected, the '84 reprised the L83 version of the venerable 5.7-liter/350-cubic-inch small-block V-8 with "Cross-Fire" dual-throttle-body fuel injection. "Cross-Fire" referred to manifolding with twin ram-air intakes that promoted more complete combustion for lower emissions. A new radiator fan and accessory drive upped horsepower and torque by five counts each to 205 hp and 290 pound-feet. All C4s built through early '84 had GM's four-speed 700-R4 Turbo Hydra-Matic with torque-converter lock-up, but the automatic soon became an optional alternative to a new "4+3 Overdrive" manual. The work of 'Vette specialist Doug Nash, this was basically a normal four-speed with a second planetary gearset, actuated by engine electronics, providing gas-saving overdrive ratios in all gears but first. The intent was improved part-throttle fuel economy—GM at the time refused to build cars that would be slapped with the government's recently enacted "gas guzzler" tax—but real-world mpg was little different from the automatic's. For best performance, OD engagement was electronically inhibited at wide throttle openings, but a manual-override switch was soon

added. The 4+3 came with a 3.07:1 rear axle (versus 2.73 for the slushbox), but 3.31:1 gearing was available for quicker launches.

In line with development goals, the C4 was the first Corvette to employ unitized construction instead of body-on-frame. This involved an upper "birdcage" structure welded to a "backbone" chassis *a la* Britain's Lotus. The latter featured a stiff C-section longitudinal beam that opened up cockpit room by eliminating two crossmembers and allowing the exhaust system to run beneath the driveshaft instead of beside it. The "birdcage" formed the windshield and door frames, lower A-pillars, rocker panels, rear cockpit wall, and front subframe. It also included a "hoop" above and behind the cockpit for added rigidity and as a hinge point for the lift-up backlight. Fully galvanized for corrosion resistance, the "uniframe," as Chevy called this structure, served as a skeleton for attaching outer body panels, which remained fiberglass, of course.

McLellan's crew used this stiffer platform to improve handling precision. The double-A-arm front suspension replaced individual coil springs with a single transverse plastic leaf. At the rear, Duntov's three-link geometry gave way to a more-sophisticated five-link setup comprising upper and lower longitudinal links, twin lateral strut rods from differential to hub carriers, and the usual tie rods, halfshafts, and transverse plastic leaf spring. Steering switched from recirculating-ball to the preferred rack-and-pinion and was quicker to boot. Ventilated four-wheel disc brakes continued but were a new lightweight, aluminum-intensive design with larger rotors. Tires were Goodyear's new ultra-sticky Eagle VR50s with unidirectional "gatorback" tread, worn on wide cast-alloy wheels.

The C4 used more lightweight materials than previous Corvettes (including beautiful aluminum forgings for suspension components). As a result, the '84 weighed some 150 pounds less than a comparable '82—around 3200 at the curb—though that was 300 pounds above the engineering target.

On the other hand, the '84 offered more standard comfort and luxury features than any previous Corvette and correspondingly fewer options. Among the latter: cruise control, power driver's seat, oil cooler, and a Z51 Performance Handling Package with upgraded springs, shocks, and front/rear antiroll bars, plus quick-ratio steering. Unfortunately, every C4 came with a dazzling digital/graphic electronic gauge cluster that was hard to read, especially on sunny days. A harsh ride—even harsher with the Z51 option—betrayed surprising structural flex. Also drawing barbs was a record base price: $23,360. But this was about all anyone could fault. Few sports cars could rival the Corvette for dynamic ability or "bang for the buck." Buyers evidently agreed. Helped by the early intro, model-year production roared back to near the '79 level, ending at 51,547.

The 1985 C4s boasted a much-revised V-8, renamed L98, with higher compression, engine oil cooler, and more-sophisticated "Tuned Port"

Both pages: **Introduced as a "targa" coupe with one-piece lift-off roof panel and lift-up rear window, the C4 was lower and wider but quite a bit shorter than the "Shark," yet was also roomier despite a wheelbase that was two inches shorter. Styling, supervised by Jerry Palmer, was less flamboyant than the Shark's. Retired GM design chief Bill Mitchell termed the C4 a grouper fish by comparison. The '84 was usefully lighter yet structurally stiffer and had a new "clamshell" hood/front-fender assembly that provided superb access to the engine and other components. This car was delivered to Consumer Guide® for testing back in the day.**

injection with individual squirters for each cylinder. Horsepower jumped by 25 to 230, while torque swelled by 40 pound-feet to 290. Customer feedback prompted softer standard and optional suspensions and the addition of gas-pressurized shock absorbers. Acceleration improved with the added power and unchanged weight, the typical 0–60-mph time sliced from 7.9 seconds to 7 flat. Base price went the other way, going to $24,403, and sales suffered, dropping nearly 23 percent to 39,729, the lowest in a decade.

Chevy kept on honing for 1986, shaving some 125 pounds from curb weight, adding an electronic anti-theft ignition key, and adopting the Bosch antilock brake system, then a novelty found mainly on much-costlier cars. The V-8 gained aluminum cylinder heads and a dual-exhaust system to reach 235 hp, but the lighter heads weren't available until midyear, so most '86s had iron heads and 230 bhp. A center high-mount rear stoplamp was added per federal decree.

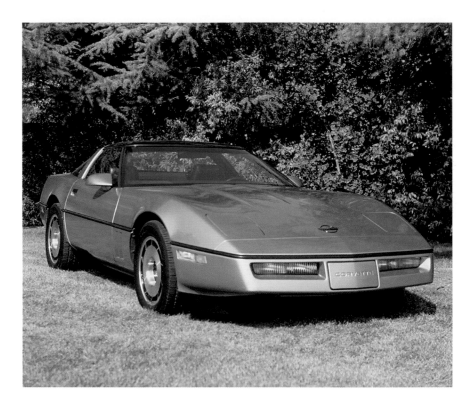

Both pages: For its sophomore year, the C4 had an improved 350 small-block V-8 dubbed L98 and featured a more-efficient multipoint "Tuned Port Injection" system that replaced the former twin-point "Cross-Fire" throttle-body setup. The new system also brought an engine cooler and higher compression. Horsepower rose by 25, to 230, and torque swelled by 40 pound-feet, to 290. New front-fender badging announced the TPI system. Performance improved, with 0–60 mph taking nearly a second less than before, at 7 flat. Styling was predictably unchanged. A four-lamp tail treatment preserved a visual link with 1968–72 Corvettes.

But the big event of 1986 was the return of the 'Vette convertible after a 10-year absence. Conveniently, it arrived in time to be selected Indianapolis 500 pace car, and all '86 ragtops were designated Pace Car Replicas. The C4 had been designed with a convertible in mind, so structural stiffening was straightforward. An X-member below the floorpan and reinforcements around the cockpit added only 50 pounds and made the shell stiffer than the coupe's. The top was manual, but few seemed to mind. Not so the convertible's $5000 price premium over the coupe, which now started at $27,000. Partly because of that, sales slipped again, this time to 34,937, of which 7264 were convertibles.

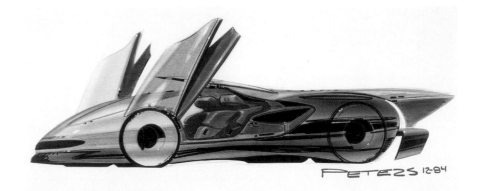

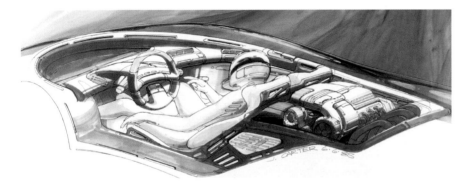

Opposite, bottom: Sun-lovers welcomed the new-for-1986 C4 convertible, the first factory ragtop Corvette in ten years. It was announced in time for Indy 500 pace-car duty; all 7264 retail units were "pace car replicas." The C4 had been engineered to go topless, so the convertible needed little structural reinforcement and weighed only 50 pounds more than the coupe. *Opposite top and this page:* GM still had mid-engine dreams and pulled out all the stops with the 1986 Corvette Indy concept. Begun in late 1984 and completed in less than a year, it ran with a 5.7-liter V-8 with special twincam cylinder heads, plus all-wheel drive, four-wheel steering, "active" suspension, and a slinky unibody made of high-tech carbon fiber. In 1988, the car was changed from silver to red and fitted with a prototype 2.65-liter V-8 that Chevy planned to make available for Indycar racing.

Ragtop sales improved to 10,625 for 1987, but total volume slid once more, to 30,632. The year's main technical change was roller valve lifters that boosted engine outputs to 240 hp and 345 pound-feet of torque. Also new was a Z52 handling package, basically a softer version of the Z51 option. An available tire-pressure monitor was announced but would be delayed until 1989.

Model-year 1988 marked Corvette's 35th anniversary, and Chevy celebrated with a $4795 trim-and-equipment option, RPO Z01. Available only for coupes, it was done mostly in white—including interior and even nameplates—accented by black roof pillars and a blue-tint glass roof

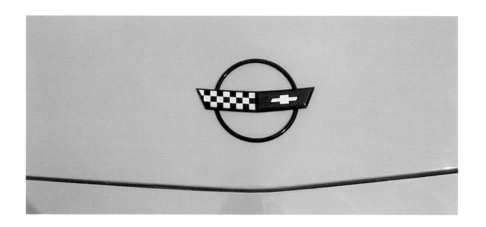

Both pages: The fourth-generation 'Vette evolved cautiously after 1984. That, plus new import competition and yearly inflation-fueled price hikes, explain Corvette's sales slide through 1988. This convertible is from 1986, when further engine tweaks boosted outputs to 240 hp and 345 pound-feet. C4 interiors (below) offered 6-footer room and comfort, but the high doorsills that contributed to structural stiffness also made for awkward entry/exit. The dashboard used through 1989 was a busy affair festooned with digital instruments that most drivers found difficult to read at a glance. On the plus side, the C4 ragtop offered no power-top option because it didn't need one, as the roof was super-easy to manually move up and down.

panel. Also included were automatic climate control, heated rear window and door mirrors, and a Sport Handling Package with 17-inch alloy wheels wearing fat P275/40ZR Goodyear Eagle tires. Just 2050 such cars were built. The larger rims were a new option for other '88s, and the standard 16-inch wheels were restyled. The suspension was modified to better resist rear-end squat in full-bore acceleration and nosedive in panic braking, which was now handled by larger, thicker four-wheel discs with dual-piston front calipers. Freer-breathing heads and a reprofiled camshaft lifted horsepower to 245 (torque was unchanged). Though production of America's sports car was now approaching a grand total of 900,000, C4 sales continued to slide, dropping to 22,789 (including 7407 ragtops), the worst showing since 1971.

In 1989, Chevrolet ended months of fevered press speculation by unveiling an all-out "King of the Hill" Corvette at the Geneva Auto Salon in Switzerland, the first time GM had premiered a domestic product outside the U.S. Though eventually postponed to the 1990 model year, the new ZR-1 was worth waiting for—if you could afford it. With a starting price of $58,995, it was the costliest car in GM history.

Available only in coupe form (technically as a $27,016 option group), the ZR-1 packed an all-new, all-aluminum V-8 engine designated LT5. It was still a 350, but with a smaller bore and longer stroke than the L98's—plus dual overhead camshafts actuating four valves per cylinder. Premium features abounded: forged-steel crankshaft and connecting rods, die-cast pistons, stellite-faced valves, sequential port fuel injection, "Direct Fire" all-coil ignition, high 11.25:1 compression, and more. The result was 375 hp and 370 pound-feet of torque, astounding numbers for an emissions-controlled street engine claimed to deliver up to 22.5 mpg. Unique to the LT5 was three-stage throttle control providing "stepped" power delivery via the electronic control module. To keep lesser-skilled—or unauthorized—drivers from getting into trouble, a special key was needed to access all 375 horses. Weighing just 39 pounds more than the L98 despite having 60

Both pages: Corvette reigned as Showroom Stock champ in Sports Car Club of America racing from 1985 to 1987. Such one-car dominance worried SCCA officials, so they asked Chevrolet to sponsor a special Corvette Challenge series as an added attraction for competitors and fans. Staged in 1988 and '89, the races allowed limited modifications, as seen here. The idea was to promote closer, more exciting races that focused on driver skill instead of on costly suspension and powertrain engineering that might preclude some teams from entering. Televised on the then-new Speedvision cable channel, Corvette Challenge proved very popular but too expensive to justify continued backing from Chevy. Even so, some of these C4s competed in 1990's New World Challenge series and have since become prized collector's items.

percent more muscle, the LT5 was carefully engineered to fit the stock C4 engine bay. As a result, the ZR-1's main visual distinctions were limited to square taillights and subtly bulged bodywork. The latter spread 74 inches wide (versus 71 for lesser models) and was needed to accommodate broader, 61.9-inch front and rear tracks.

ZR-1 production was initially pegged at 4000–5000 per year, low volume that made it more practical for Chevrolet to source the LT5 engine from Oklahoma-based Mercury Marine. The car itself, however, was built on the regular Corvette line at Bowling Green.

Meantime, regular 1989 Corvettes benefited from two other ZR-1 features. One was a six-speed manual gearbox designed by Chevy and Germany's ZF. Besides pulling a tighter rear-axle ratio (3.33:1), it had vastly better shift action than the never-liked "4+3" it replaced. It also had a rather odd thing called computer-aided gear selection (CAGS) that "forced" a 1–4 shift at light throttle between 12 and 19 mph—another oddity dictated by government fuel-economy test procedures. But though CAGS seemed to spoil the fun, it rarely intruded in the kind of leadfoot driving done by most 'Vette owners.

Both pages: Though again visibly unchanged outside, the 1988 Corvettes received a number of suspension upgrades that improved the C4's already stellar handling abilities. Also making news were beefier brakes, another round of engine tweaks that lifted horsepower to 245, and a 35th Anniversary option package that attracted 2050 orders. This was the last year for the C4's novel "4+3" manual transmission, which was basically a regular 4-speed with an extra planetary gearset comprising a trio of electronically controlled overdrive gears. Designed to maximize fuel economy—and avoid the federal "gas guzzler" tax—this gearbox was rather cumbersome to use, which explains why most C4s through '88 were sold with the base 4-speed overdrive automatic. Total C4 sales hit a new model-year low for the generation at just under 23,000.

Corvette's second 1989 innovation was Selective Ride Control (RPO FX3), restricted to cars with the new six-speed and the Z51 handling package. Like some Japanese setups, this electromechanical system provided three driver-selectable damping levels—Touring, Sport, and Competition—via electric motors that varied the size of the proportioning-valve orifice in each shock absorber. Each level also contained six progressively firmer settings that automatically cut in with increasing speed to promote optimum handling. Developed by Bilstein and GM's Delco Division, SRC was claimed to improve both ride and cornering. It

did, but not dramatically. Many aficionados claim that SRC is the single most important "dynamic" option of the period.

Other '89 developments included standardizing the 17-inch wheel/ tire option and a modified Z52 handling package. The latter included a strengthened front chassis section (introduced with the '86 convertible), faster-ratio steering, Delco/Bilstein gas-filled shocks, and, for six-speed cars, engine-oil cooler, heavy-duty radiator, and auxiliary cooling fan. Finally, rearranged top latches made the convertible more-convenient, and Chevy returned to tradition by offering a detachable hardtop for it

Both pages: Enthusiasts applauded two new performance options for 1989: a 6-speed manual transmission and Selective Ride Control—electromechanical shock absorbers that varied firmness within three driver-chosen settings. Last but not least among changes for '89 was Chevy's revival of a detachable hardtop option. Conveniently, it was designed to fit 1986–88 models, too. The car pictured here is running without its wheels' center caps.

(priced at $2000 and retro-fittable to 1986–88 models). Though prices kept climbing—to $31,545 for the coupe and near $37K for the convertible—Corvette sales went up for a change, rising by some 3600 units to 26,412 (including 9749 ragtops).

Two laudable standard safety features arrived for 1990: a driver-side airbag (hidden in the steering-wheel hub) and an improved "ABS II" braking system. The latter was especially worthwhile on the ZR-1, which could do 0–60 mph in a blistering 4.5 seconds, the standing quarter-mile in 13.4 at 108.5 mph, and top 175 mph. A more debatable improvement was a new "aircraft-inspired" instrument panel for all '90 'Vettes, a planned change that contributed to the ZR-1's delay (as did an early lack of engines). The redone dash replaced most of the previous digi-graphic displays with easy-read analog gauges but was less user-friendly than it might have been and looked rather cheap, especially in the pricey ZR-1.

To Chevrolet's chagrin, Corvette sales turned down again for 1990, sagging to 23,646 (including 7630 convertibles). The onset of yet another sharp recession played a part, but so did relentless price escalation. The standard coupe now started at $32,000, the convertible at more than $37,000. The ZR-1 drew just 3049 orders, fewer than Chevy's projected 4000-unit minimum—and more's the pity. With its world-class powertrain and spectacular performance, the King was a technical triumph for GM and an international sensation, the cover story for car magazines on four continents. And because it looked a surefire collector's item, rabid speculators and fools with money gladly paid more than $100,000 for early examples. Yet within 18 months, ZR-1s were selling for well under sticker amid reports of surplus engines and rumors that the model would soon be dropped.

Sales-wise, fate had been curiously unkind to the most technically advanced and capable Corvette generation yet. But the C4 was far from finished, as we'll see in the next chapter.

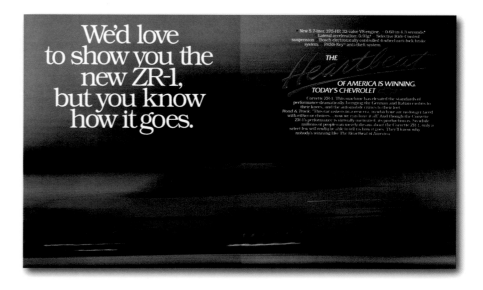

Both pages: A rumored "King of the Hill" Corvette was announced in 1989 as the ZR-1 but went on sale as a 1990 coupe-only model with a new dash and minor exterior differences from the pre-production car seen here. For the costliest 'Vette to that time—nearly $59,000—the ZR-1 was curiously hard to distinguish from other C4s: just fatter tires and a body three inches wider with squarish taillamps. What ZR-1 buyers really wanted was the exclusive new all-aluminum, twincam, multivalve V-8 by Mercury Marine with 375 hp and 370 pound-feet of torque. Zero to 60: 5 seconds.

With GM's fortunes fading, Corvette had to stand pat for another season. One executive stood firm against dilution of the brand, and fans from around the world embraced the new National Corvette Museum.

1991–1996: GM TO CORVETTE: BE PATIENT

America's sports car was nearly killed off in 1954, and it came close to death again in the early 1990s. Why? Basically because General Motors was not the all-powerful company it had been 40 years before. Though still America's largest automaker, GM had been losing market share and tons of money—a disturbing $18 billion net from 1990 to 1993. One problem, many analysts said, was that GM had too many factories with the capacity to build too many vehicles for too few customers. And where Detroit rivals Ford and Chrysler had been forced to become leaner, more efficient, and more responsive to ever-stronger import-brand competition, GM remained a slow-moving, bureaucratic behemoth saddled with the U.S. industry's highest overhead and lowest profit margins—plus an unshakable belief in its own infallibility.

In the midst of that unfortunate corporate hubris, though, Corvette refused to be changed into something that was other than purely Corvette. Company accountants and even some people in Chevy marketing convinced themselves that a smaller, or cheaper, or lighter, or less powerful Corvette wouldn't simply save the marque, but jump-start a flow of dollars into GM's coffers. But others inside GM said No.

The river of red ink triggered a top-level management shakeup in 1992 that soon led many new-model programs to be scratched or delayed. The C5 Corvette, in the works since the late '80s, received extra-close scrutiny in light of the C4's generally disappointing sales to date. At one point there was serious talk of killing the 'Vette despite its image and commercial value as a performance icon and Chevrolet Division's flagship car. After GM's typical myriad committee meetings and some political intrigue, it was decided to cancel a proposed 1995 "reskin" and to revive the $250-million C5 program. Though the 'Vette had been spared, the C5 was eventually pushed back to 1997, thus extending the C4 run by three years. Many fans were disappointed, but Corvette development carried on.

Both pages: Mainstream Corvettes got a mild facelift for 1991—but so did the ZR-1, as Chevrolet inexplicably missed an opportunity to give the "King of the Hill" a greater visual distinction beyond a wider body and retention of a roof-mounted high-center stoplamp (other '91s moved that into the back panel). The lack of styling pop and a steep price figured in the ZR-1's steady sales decline after its debut year. So did competition from the new V-10 Dodge Viper and added power newly available with other Corvettes. Chevy tried to bolster the King's fortunes for '93 by adding 30 horses for a Viper-matching 405, but sales continued to slide. Corvette's '91 facelift also introduced a new dashboard (above right and page 125) with analog instead of bar-graph minor gauges and a more coherent layout, but the design still suffered from "buttonitis."

Meantime, and as planned, the fourth-generation got its first styling changes for 1991, a mild facelift that freshened appearance just enough to be noticeable. Included were a smoother, slimmer front fascia with wrapped turn-signal/fog-lamp assemblies and front fenders with four horizontal "strakes" instead of twin "gills." But to the outrage of those who'd rushed to lay out big bucks for ZR-1s, standard models also got a King-like

convex back panel and square taillights, albeit with no change in overall width. Though Chevy never explained this move, the likely motive was to boost overall Corvette sales with ZR-1 style. If so, the plan backfired, as model-year volume slipped by some 3000 units to 20,646. Of these, a mere 2044 were ZR-1s (versus 3049 the previous season).

Record prices again loomed large in that year's sales retreat. The

Both pages: These images from the GM Design Staff archives show a mildly customized '91 convertible that was likely the "company" car of designer Jerry Palmer (opposite), who at that time headed GM's Advanced Concept Center in Southern California. Palmer had supervised styling of the 1984 C4 as Chief Designer in the Chevrolet III Studio. He was also the lead designer of the memorable 1972 "Four-Rotor" mid-engine concept that grew out of the XP-882 program of the early Seventies. And Palmer supervised styling development of Chevy's third-generation Camaro, which arrived for 1982, not long before the fourth-generation 'Vette. Palmer, now retired, has always been an avid "car guy."

Both pages: Reeves Callaway of Old Lyme, Connecticut, was a respected engineer who devised a twin-turbo conversion of Corvette's L98 V-8 (below, center) in 1988 that Chevy offered as a fully warranted Regular Production Option (RPO) B2K. After the L98 was dropped, Callaway finalized his ultimate Twin Turbo, the one-off Sledgehammer (both pages), which set a world speed record of 254.76 mph in 1988. Callaway marketed the drag-reducing lower-body panels as an "aerobody" kit for post-sale installation. A total of 497 Twin Turbos were built for 1987–91. Note the four-point racing belts and cold-air hood.

ZR-1 option now added $31,683 to the normal coupe's base price, which was up to $32,455; the convertible started at $38,770. Mechanical changes were of the detail sort: a standard power-steering cooler, a new Z07 package combining the F×3 and Z51 options (still available separately), first-time F×3 availability for the convertible, and a "retained power" feature that allowed operating accessories for a few minutes after shutting off the engine.

Dave Hill took over as Corvette chief engineer in September 1992.

He was a good choice, having played the same role for Cadillac's ill-starred 1988–93 Allanté. Hill was no less committed than Dave McLellan to traditional Corvette values, including rear drive and a unique platform. But with two-seater sales increasingly tough—and with GM in such turmoil—he also knew that Corvette would have to "pull its own weight" as never before. That meant not only increasing sales but making each one more profitable by taking cost out of the car—without spoiling it, of course. GM had lately been thinking about spinning future 'Vettes from a lower-cost,

Both pages: The Callaway twin Turbo Corvette went out in stunning style with this racy Speedster, of which a mere 10 were produced in 1991. Designed by Paul Deutschman, it combined a version of his "Aerobody" panels (mostly mounted below the perimeter "rub line") with a cutdown windshield and sloped, faired-in headrests. Priced from $107,00—then a king's ransom—the Callaway Speedster packed 450 horses and a stout 600 pound-feet of torque.

higher-volume platform, but Hill wouldn't have it. As he told the press in 1993: "I can assure you, the last thing on our minds is a hot version of the Camaro replacing the Corvette."

As if to signal continued faith in its sports car, Chevy again reworked the hallowed small-block V-8 for 1992 to give base Corvettes an extra 50 horsepower, 300 in all. Titled LT1, the rejuvenated engine was also quicker to wind out and had a higher rev limit, though it wasn't as torquey as the L98, with 330 pound-feet peaking at 4000 rpm (versus 340 at 3200). Nevertheless, the LT1 was cheered by the press and enthusiasts alike, many of whom felt that it rendered the ZR-1 almost superfluous. And with its 5.4-second 0–60-mph capability, the LT1 'Vette wasn't that much slower

than the King, especially considering the huge dollar difference—which widened a bit, as ZR-1 pricing was unchanged and the base coupe rose to $33,465. The convertible was up to $40,145 before options.

The ZR-1 itself added front-fender nameplates for '92, and all Corvettes now boasted Acceleration Slip Regulation, a new Bosch-designed traction-control system. Like similar setups at Porsche, BMW, and Mercedes, ASR used the ABS sensors to detect wheelspin, in which event it would either brake the offending wheels and/or throttle back power to keep you from slip-sliding away. To back it up, all '92s wore grippier tires, Goodyear's new asymmetric-tread Eagle GS-C.

Those tires grew wider on standard '93s and wider aft than fore.

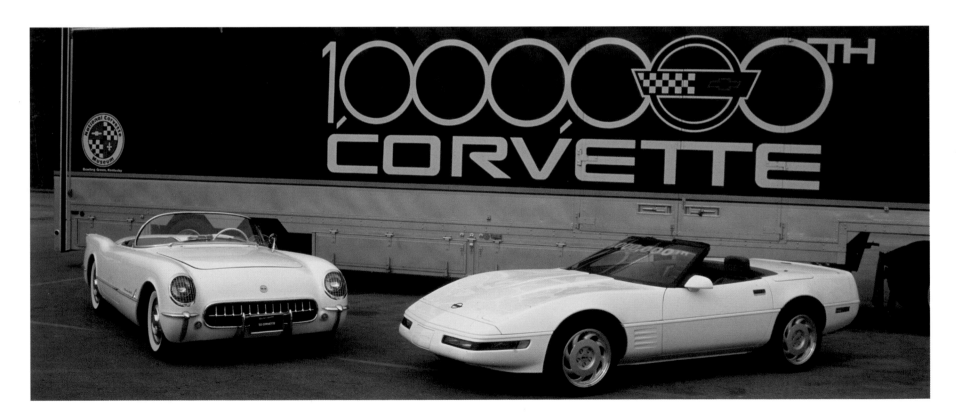

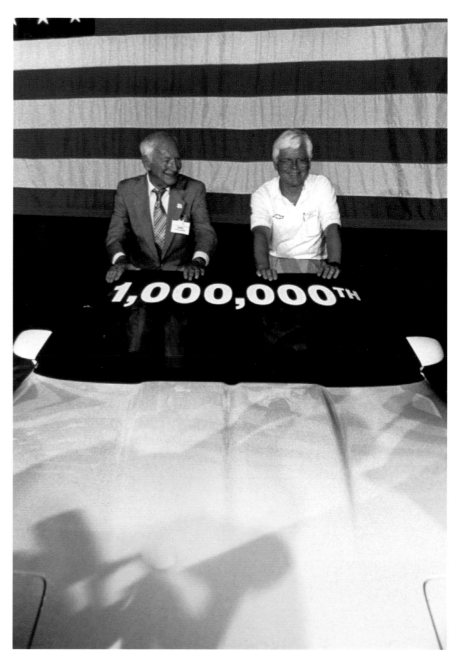

Both pages: Chevy marked production of the one-millionth Corvette on July 2, 1992. Doubtless by design, the milestone car was a white '92 convertible bearing one-of-a-kind trim detail. It made a natural photo op with an original '53 (opposite) at the Bowling Green, Kentucky, site of the National Corvette Museum, which would open in 1994. Many GM luminaries were on hand for the occasion, notably (above right) legendary Corvette chief engineer Zora Arkus-Duntov (left) and his successor, David R. McLellan.

Both pages: The big Corvette news for 1992 was yet another upgrade of the ever-green 350-cid 5.7-liter small-block V-8. Dubbed LT1, the tweaked motor rated a healthy 300 horsepower and 330 pound-feet of torque via higher compression, computer-controlled engine timing, and freer-flow cylinder heads and exhaust. Though still running with 75 fewer horses than the vaunted ZR-1, an LT1 was only a little slower in the 0–60 dash: 5.1 seconds versus 4.7—and it cost thousands less. This car's badging and license plate note RPO Z07, a new-for-'91 combination of the Z51 and FX3 suspension options aimed mainly at racers and hardcore driving enthusiasts. Traction control was newly standard for all '92s.

In fact, they were now close to King-size: at the back, 285/40ZR17s on 9.5-inch-wide rims; in front, 255/45ZR17s on 8.5s. Also for '93, the LT1 was retuned to deliver 340 pound-feet of torque, up 10 (hp was unchanged). The LT5 was massaged as well, internal changes boosting it to 405 hp at 5800 rpm (up 30) and torque to 385 pound-feet at 5200 (plus 15). With that, the ZR-1 was again the power king of American production cars after bowing to Dodge's spartan new Viper RT/10 in 1991–92.

Unfortunately, the extra muscle didn't do much for the King's 0–60 kick—about 0.2-second at most, according to *Car and Driver*'s tests. Top speed, however, was up to a shattering 179, and the new tires improved skidpad cornering from 0.88g to a race-carlike 0.92. Yet all this was quite academic, for ZR-1 sales were down to a trickle now: a mere 448 for '93 versus 502 the previous season. On the other hand, total Corvette sales went up for the first time in four years. Though the gain was only a little more than 1000 units, the '93 tally of 21,590 was heartening particularly because this was Corvette's 40th year.

Yes, it was birthday time again and, as expected, Chevrolet issued another anniversary special. A $1455 package option available for any '93, it comprised Ruby Red paint and wheel centers, a color-matched leather-trimmed interior, embroidered "40th" logos on headrests, and corresponding bright insignia on nose, deck, and front fenders. Available separately was a new gadget, the Passive Keyless Entry system. This used a pair of small transmitters to generate a low-power electromagnetic field within a few feet of the car's perimeter; walking up to or away from the car interrupted the field to lock or unlock the doors and hatch. It was a gimmick worthy of Cadillac, Mercedes, or luxury-class upstart Lexus, but only Corvette had it. Of course, the 'Vette had been picking up such doodads for years, yet even the posh '93 was still no less the red-blooded all-American sports car loved by millions all over the world.

A good many of those folks got together in September 1994 for a genuine lovefest: the opening of the National Corvette Museum.

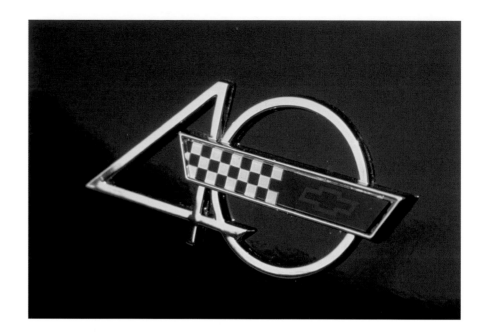

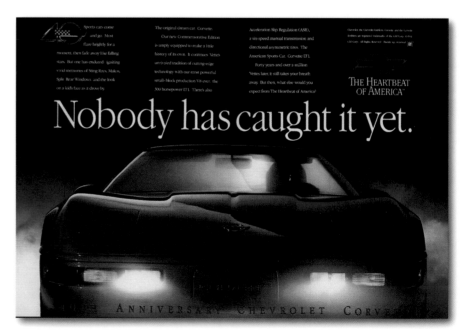

Opposite: To no one's surprise, Chevy marked Corvette's 40th anniversary with a special trim package that dressed '93 models with celebratory logos, Ruby Red paint, and a color-keyed leather interior. The option showed up on 6749 of the total 21,590 Corvettes built for that model year. *This page, above:* Base '93s joined the ZR1 in having staggered-width wheels, with the fronts narrowed an inch to 8.5; rear rims were still 9.5 inches, but carried slightly wider tires. *Right:* Unveiled at the 1992 Detroit Auto Show, the Sting Ray III concept hinted at a smaller, lighter future Corvette. Standing two inches shorter than a C4 on a 102-inch wheelbase, it used a modified LT1 V-8 up front and a rear-mounted transmission. Though it didn't influence the next 'Vette, Sting Ray II provided broad clues to Chevy's upcoming 1993 Camaro.

Located in Bowling Green, Kentucky, not far from the factory, this shrine to America's sports car was built with private funds and no initial blessing from Chevrolet. But the division soon recognized it as—ahem—a concrete expression of Corvette fandom and thus a potential gold mine of corporate goodwill. Accordingly, Chevy raided its attic for exhibits, making "permanent loans" of various historic Corvettes, engines, and other memorabilia, including Bill Mitchell's 1959 Sting Ray racer and 1965 Mako Shark II show car. Zora Duntov was persuaded to attend the museum's opening ceremonies, as was Dave McLellan. Both were doubtless moved by the sight of some 2000 vintage Corvettes driven in from around the U.S., and a few foreign countries, by loyal owners who just had to be present for a signal moment in automotive history.

Chevy, meantime, cheered a second consecutive gain in Corvette volume, the '94s attracting 23,330 sales despite few changes. Still, the

updates were timely and useful. For starters, the dash was modified to accommodate knee bolsters and—per federal "passive restraint" rules—a passenger-side airbag. Steering wheel, seats, and door panels were revised, and convertibles gained a standard heated-glass backlight. The four-speed automatic transmission adopted electronic shift control (for smoother gear changes) and a safety-shift interlock (to forestall "unintended acceleration"). The LT1 received a few more minor refinements, but outputs stood pat. ZR-1s wore new-design five-spoke wheels, the optional FX3 suspension got slightly softer damping, and a new and more-effective ABS/traction-control system was standardized. Joining the options list were Goodyear "run-flat" tires, which could be driven safely for up to 50 miles without air. The ZR-1 package was downpriced a bit to $31,258 but managed only 448 orders.

Both pages: After a successful Corvette racing career in the Sixties and early Seventies, John Greenwood set up shop in Florida with his brother Burt. They devised a series of limited-edition, high-performance 'Vettes with wild aerodynamic styling, trackworthy chassis enhancements, and turbocharged V-8s. The ultimate Greenwood C4 was this one-off G-572 from the early Nineties. Named for its target horsepower, it was theoretically capable of 3-second 0–60-mph sprints and low-11 quarter-mile blasts.

The King was belatedly buried after 1995 and a final 448 examples. It would have died sooner, but Chevy had agreed to buy a minimum number of LT5 engines from supplier Mercury Marine, and the condition was only satisfied that year. Other '95 Corvettes got the ZR-1's heavy-duty brakes as standard, plus revised fender "gills" and, on automatic models, a transmission-fluid temperature gauge. Base prices kept climbing, but the $36,785 coupe and $43,665 ragtop were not outrageously expensive, considering their performance and standard features. A comparable BMW, Jaguar, or Mercedes-Benz cost thousands more.

A near-stock LT1 convertible paced the 1995 Indy 500, the third such honor for Corvette and the 10th for a Chevrolet. Predictably, Chevy ran off a few replicas: exactly 527 this time, of which 87 were used by "dignitaries" on race day, 20 exported, and the rest doled out to Chevy's top-performing U.S. dealers. All were painted Dark Purple Metallic over Arctic White and came with "79th Indianapolis 500" decals for owner application, plus embroidered logos on the seats. The rather striking $2816 option was

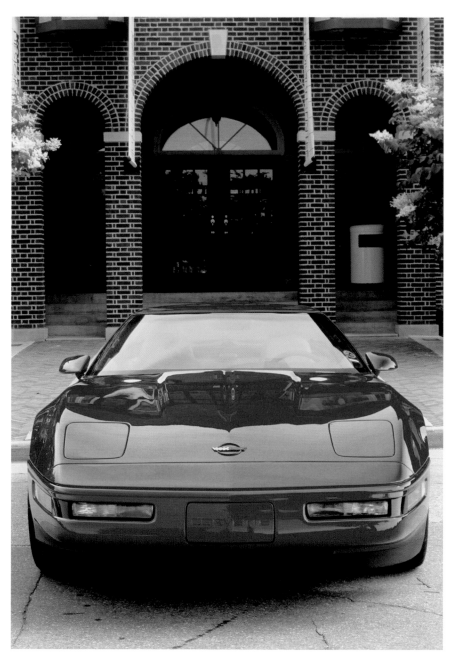

Both pages: Chevrolet initially expected to sell 4000–5000 ZR-1s each year but ended up building only 6939 over the six-year run that ended with model-year 1995. Stiff pricing and ever-faster base Corvettes hastened its demise, but so did high manufacturing costs, relentless new "supercar" competition, and, toward the end, the start of work on the next-generation Corvette. But though the ZR-1 was a commercial disappointment, it was a high-water mark for GM engineering and a fascinating chapter in the saga of America's sports car. And the "King" did have its day, setting 12 world speed and endurance records in 1990 that would not be broken for 11 years.

available for both body styles, though it naturally excluded the actual pace cars' light bar and other track-required equipment.

Magazine testers had been noticing steady improvements in Corvette workmanship and ride comfort, and the '95s were the best yet. Though Chevy couldn't seem to exorcise certain squeaks and rattles, the fourth generation was by now acceptably tight and solid on rough roads, which no longer chattered your teeth so much.

With the replacement C5 nearing completion, the C4 took a final bow for 1996. Chevy bid it farewell in fine style, starting with another Collector Edition, a $1250 package that dressed-up either body style

with pearlescent Sebring Silver paint, bright five-spoke alloys, and special emblems and trim.

More intriguing was a new limited-edition Grand Sport package (RPO Z16), a successor of sorts to the ZR-1. Priced at $3250 for coupes and $2880 for convertibles, it included the King's wheels and tires, plus showy black brake calipers, a pair of red "hashmarks" on the left fender, and, for coupes, tacked-on but tasteful rear-wheel-arch extensions. A specific color scheme combined Admiral Blue paint with a broad, white dorsal stripe, recalling the trio of original GS Sting Rays raced by John Mecom at Nassau in '63.

Both pages: In 1995, Corvette again answered the call to Indy 500 pace car duty—after Chevy wangled an invitation. By this time, years of mechanical and suspension work had produced a C4 that needed few modifications for race day, so the actual pace convertible was basically stock except for a track-required roll bar and exterior warning lights, plus the usual special paint job and graphics. Shown here is one of the 527 cars built with the Z4Z Pace Car Replica package, which was available on coupes and convertibles. Of those replicas, 87 served at Indy or for PR, 20 were exported, and the remaining 415 were sold through Chevy's top-performing dealers.

But the Grand Sport's big attraction was its new LT4 engine. Optional for other '96s at $1450, this was essentially an LT1 with wider ports, bigger valves with hollow stems and stronger springs, reshaped pistons giving 10.8:1 compression (versus 10.4), wilder cam, high-flow fuel injectors, and a sturdier crank. The result was 330 horsepower peaking at a higher 5800 rpm, plus an extra five extra pound-feet of torque (340 total).

Rounding out GS features were six-way power sport seats with embroidered "Grand Sport" logos and a leather-lined interior in all-black or black and blinding red. Trivia hounds should note that the coupe's lift-off roof-panel option was *verboten* with the GS group, and that white was the only top color for GS convertibles. Available for all '96s was new "Selective Real-Time Damping," essentially a faster-acting F×3 setup priced at $1695.

GS production was quite low: 810 coupes and just 190 convertibles. But total Corvette sales inched up to 21,536, so at least the C4 exited on a positive note.

Both pages: The C4 enjoyed a last hur-rah with the limited-edition 1996 Grand Sport, a one-year-only performance package available for coupe and con-vertible. Just 1000 were built, with coupes likely in the majority. Admiral Blue paint with white dorsal racing stripes recalled the classic Sting Ray-based GS of the Sixties. An exclusive and much-modified V-8, dubbed LT4, delivered 330 hp, 30 more than the stock LT1, plus a higher redline. Other features included mandatory 6-speed manual transmission, ZR-1 wheels and tires, a unique suspension, bold red hash marks on the front fenders, rear-fender flares, and a black or red/black interior with a serial-number plaque.

A Fresh Slate, a Few Bugs,
and the Return of the Ragtop.

1997-2004: LEAN AND MEAN

The first Corvette with virtually no ties to previous models—or any other car—was created by a new generation of General Motors talents led by chief engineer Dave Hill, assistant chief engineer John Heinricy, and chief designer John Cafaro. Chief goals for the C5 were improved workmanship, structural rigidity, operating efficiency, and interior space; reduced production costs; and wider market appeal with an overall design based heavily on consumer "focus group" input.

Delayed some four years by GM's early-1990s financial woes, the C5 boasted altered dimensions on an innovative new unibody structure. Wheelbase grew a whopping 8.3 inches to a Corvette-record 104.5, width swelled nearly three inches to 73.6, and height rose 1.4 inches

to 47.7. Even so, the C5 was only 1.2 inches longer than the C4 at 179.7, and actually weighed some 80 pounds less in initial hatch coupe form. Beneath the slinky new fiberglass body—with a lower, 0.29 drag factor—was a much-stiffer frame with a massive "backbone" tunnel and stout hydroformed siderails (die-cast by a high-pressure water process). An aluminum windshield/cowl structure connected to a pair of rectangular steel members rising from the front frame rails. A cast-magnesium steering column/pedal box added more strength with minimal weight. A new steel superstructure provided better support for the coupe's liftup rear window and takeoff roof panel, the latter now framed in magnesium and attached by latches instead of bolts and a wrench.

Despite the hefty siderails, sill height dropped four inches, making for much easier entry/exit. Footwells were usefully wider, helped by Corvette's first rear-mounted transmission, either a four-speed automatic or optional six-speed manual. This wasn't a true transaxle, as the differential remained separate, but it didn't impinge on luggage space, which more than doubled in the hatch coupe to 25 cubic feet. More

importantly, the tail-mounted gearbox helped improve fore/aft weight distribution to 51.5/48.5 percent, all the better for handling.

So, too, a raft of suspension updates. Front double A-arms continued, along with front/rear antiroll bars and plastic transverse leaf springs, but all components now mounted on noise-isolating cast-aluminum subframes. In addition, new rear A-arms with toe-control links relieved

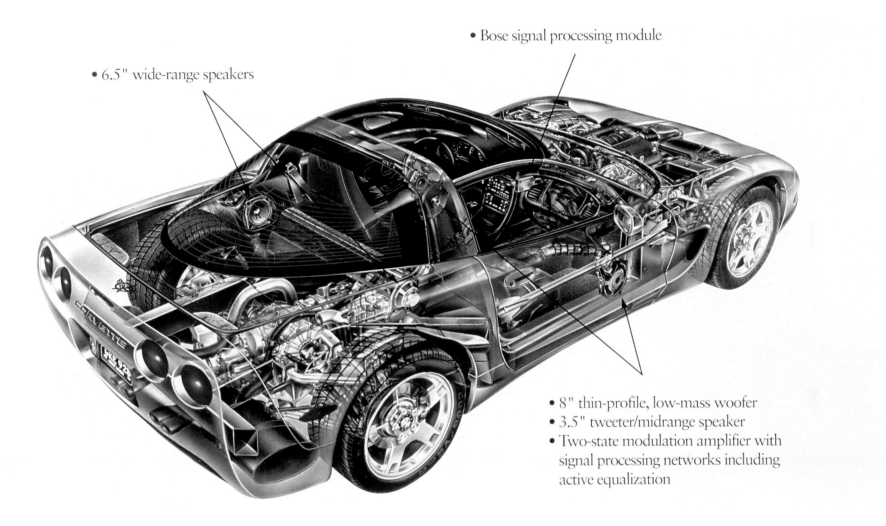

- 6.5" wide-range speakers

- Bose signal processing module

- 8" thin-profile, low-mass woofer
- 3.5" tweeter/midrange speaker
- Two-state modulation amplifier with signal processing networks including active equalization

Opposite: Work toward the C5 was underway by the late Eighties and assumed a C4-size package with swoopy lines *a la* the mid-engine Corvette Indy and CERV III concepts. Then, for various reasons, GM brass suspended the project and later reopened it, targeting 1996 for the car's debut. This C5 would be smaller and lighter, in the manner of the 1992 Sting Ray III concept; the clay seen here is one variation. *Above:* This "X-ray" view reveals the C5's rear-mounted transmission—Corvette's first—its Bose audio system, and the car's generally space-efficient packaging.

the halfshafts of suspension duty; bushings were changed all-round; and shocks were repositioned and revalved for tighter wheel control. Steering changed to GM's new computer-managed "Magnasteer II" system that varied effort according to road speed via electromagnets instead of hydraulics. All-disc antilock brakes returned, slightly smaller in diameter but thicker. Tires were resized (P245/45ZR17 front, P275/40ZR18 rear) and unique to Corvette: specially developed Goodyear Eagle F1 GS EMTs designed to "run flat" for up to 200 miles, thus eliminating the need for a weighty, space-robbing spare tire.

There was a new V-8, too. Dubbed LS1, it mimicked the LT1/LT4 only in having two overhead valves per cylinder and identical bore spacing.

Opposite, top: An undated rear-end workout suggests that C5 designers labored to reinterpret hallmark Corvette visuals in new and interesting ways. *Opposite main:* This "C-ZR1" model was built on Indy/CERV III themes. It had little influence on the production C5, but a plunging, arrow-shaped nose survived in muted form on Chevy's new-for-'93 Camaro sport coupe. *This page:* C5 styling was essentially locked in by May 1994. Camouflaged "beta" prototypes began rigorous road testing the following April, subject to everything from scorching desert heat to sloppy, high-altitude cold.

Highlights included a deeper-skirted block made of aluminum, reworked cylinder heads, freer-flow intake and exhaust systems, and Corvette's first "drive-by-wire" throttle. The last replaced the normal mechanical linkage with an electric motor that worked the throttle by computer control according to input from an accelerator-position sensor. The throttle was tied through the engine computer to standard cruise and traction control functions for precise power delivery under all conditions, plus fewer parts and easier installation.

At 346 cid, the LS1 had fewer cubes than its iron-block forebears but was lighter, physically smaller, and more potent, spinning out 345 horsepower and 350 pound-feet of torque. Even better, it rated slightly higher EPA fuel-economy numbers.

Tellingly, the C5 claimed 34 percent fewer parts than the C4 so that it would be easier to build to a higher quality standard. But no one's perfect. The first 1400 C5s were recalled for rear suspension fixes, and

early road tests noted windows that pushed away from their seals at high speed—and more pesky, unwanted squeaks and rattles.

But the rough edges were mostly smoothed out within six months, and they did nothing to dampen the C5's enthusiastic reception. Though some thought the styling a bit tame, there was no doubting the new car's ability. Most magazines timed 0–60 mph at a swift five seconds with manual shift and praised the near-flat, grippy cornering (0.85g in one test); effortless, stable, high-speed cruising; the comfortable new cabin with its refreshingly no-nonsense gauges and controls; greater on-road solidity; and, yes, better workmanship throughout. Best of all, the '97 coupe started at $37,945, just $770 above its '96 counterpart. No wonder journalist David E. Davis termed the C5 "a home run in every way...." A deliberately slow ramp-up limited 1997-model production to 9752 units, but output then jumped to 31,084, the 'Vette's best one-year performance since 1986.

The C5 was designed as a convertible first, and sun-lovers cheered

Both pages: Arriving for 1997, a year later than planned, the C5 was the first Corvette with few design or engineering ties to the car it replaced. That included not only exterior styling but cockpit design, too. There was a new 350-cid/5.7-liter V-8 as well as a lighter aluminum-block engine tagged LS1. It sent 345 horsepower and 350 pound-feet of torque through a 4-speed automatic or optional 6-speed manual transaxle. Sold only as a hatchback coupe for '97, the C5 was lighter yet stronger than the C4, and roomier.

the ragtop's return for 1998. Some groused that the top was still manual, but it was easy to operate and visibly better made. Trunk space was only about half that of the hatch coupe's but double that of the C4 convertible. And it was accessible via the 'Vette's first external trunklid since 1962. Unsurprisingly, Chevrolet got the new convertible selected as 1998 Indy 500 pace car—Corvette's fourth such honor—and rolled out replicas for retail sale, 1163 in all. *Motor Trend* had passed over the 'Vette as 1997 Car of the Year but awarded its '98 trophy to the entire Corvette "line."

Two new options arrived: magnesium wheels (soon withdrawn due to supplier problems) and, at midseason, an "Active Handling" antiskid

system. The latter supplemented the traction control with additional sensor input allowing more-precise selective braking of individual wheels to keep the car on course. Like the coupe, the convertible offered three suspension choices: base, firm-ride Z51 ($350), and an evolved F45 "Selective Real-Time Damping" option (a pricey $1695), basically computer-controlled auto-adjusting shock absorbers with driver-selectable Tour, Sport, and Performance modes. Opinion was divided on the effectiveness of these setups, but most critics thought the F45 too harsh on most roads. Consumer Guide® preferred the base calibrations, but *Car and Driver* felt the Z51 delivered better handling with little loss of ride comfort, being

Both pages: A C5 convertible was a foregone conclusion. It bowed for 1998 as a much stiffer ragtop
Corvette than the C4 version. Pace-car duty at Indy
came up again—for the fourth time—and that brought
the predictable batch of retail replicas, which this
time numbered 1158, all ragtops like this one. The
replicas differed little from the actual race-day cars
but came with many features that were optional for
other '98s. All C5 convertibles had a separate trunk
with lid, the first such for an open 'Vette since 1962!
And the 13.9-cubic-foot capacity was the best of any
contemporary convertible. The top remained manual
only but was visibly better made than the C4's and
even easier to operate.

"nowhere near as punishing as the C4 Z51 was."

That's just as well, because the Z51 was mandatory for 1999's new "hardtop" model, a fixed-roof convertible that had figured in C5 planning all along. Its mission was to double yearly Corvette sales by offering just the basics (manual cloth seats, smaller footwear, conventional suspension) at a much lower price, once whispered at around $25,000. But the idea bombed in customer "clinics" and Chevy was selling every C5 it built anyway. Accordingly, the hardtop was recast as a "pure performance" machine, sold only with manual transmission, the Z51 chassis, and few options. Chevy did restore traction control, 18-inch rolling stock, and leather upholstery; but extras were limited to the antiskid system, power driver's seat, and Bose audio.

The hardtop's roof was made of fiberglass and bonded to the convertible bodyshell. With that and fewer frills, the model aimed to be a lighter, stiffer Corvette with consequently better acceleration and handling. Stiffer it was, but it only weighed some 90 pounds less, so it was barely faster than a well-driven manual coupe or convertible. *C/D* reported 0–60 mph at 4.8 seconds, *Road & Track* a more believable 5.3. But "buff" magazines loved the hardtop. "We applaud Chevy's tactic of making the quickest Corvette the cheapest," *C/D* enthused. But the $38,171 base price was hardly budget territory, so the hardtop drew only 4031 first-year sales.

Still, it signaled that Chevy was again really serious about the Corvette. Another clue was the $3.5 million spent to develop the C5-R, an all-out racing version with a 6.0-liter V-8 making some 600 hp for an assault on the fabled 24 Hours of Le Mans. After shakedowns in several long-distance U.S. races during 2000, the C5-R made history in France the following year by placing 10th and 11th (first and second in the GTS Class), the first Le Mans finish for factory-backed 'Vettes in 40 years.

Hardtop aside, Corvette's only other 1999 news involved two new options for the coupe and convertible: a power telescopic steering column

Both pages: Model-year 1999 brought a third Corvette body style, a "hardtop" convertible with a fixed, bonded-on fiberglass roof. Developed alongside the ragtop and the hatch coupe, it was initially conceived as a no-frills entry-level 'Vette but was ultimately recast as a "pure performance" machine with mandatory manual gearbox and Z51 handling package, plus fewer comfort and convenience options that would have added unwanted pounds. First-year sales were just 12 percent of Corvette's 33,270 total—a disappointment—but Chevy had bigger plans for this model.

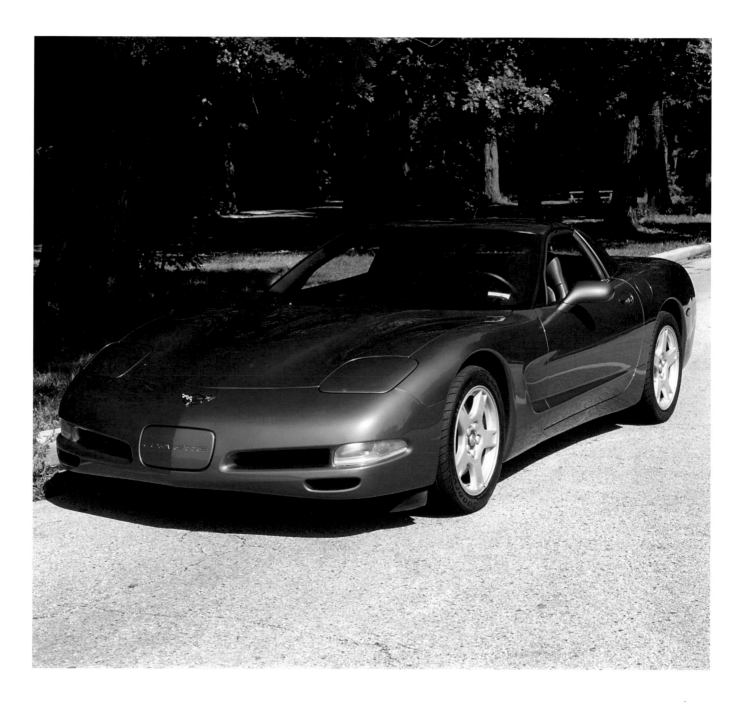

and an aircraft-style head-up display (HUD) that projected speed and other data onto the windshield at driver eye level. It could be distracting, but could also be turned off. Buyers were still turned on by the C5, as model-year production rose seven percent to 33,270.

The 2000 total was only 89 units higher, but prices weren't much higher either: $38,900 hardtop, $39,475 coupe, $45,900 convertible. The hardtop could now be optioned like other models with the HUD, dual-zone climate control, and fog lamps, but buyers were unmoved and sales plunged to 2090.

Chevy responded for 2001 by upgrading the hardtop so that it really was the fastest, best-handling Corvette. Tagged Z06, recalling the rare 1963 racing package, it boasted a heavily reworked V-8 reviving another legendary RPO: LS6. Higher compression, hotter cam, new heads, and

smoother, higher-capacity intake and exhaust helped extract 385 hp and 385 pound-feet, up 40 hp and 35 pound-feet from the previous LS1. The LS1 itself got some of the same refinements to add five hp and 25 pound-feet for totals of 350 and 375. To match Z06 power, engineers specified a stronger six-speed gearbox, a firmer FE4 suspension, thicker antiroll bars, and wider wheels and tires. The purpose-designed Goodyear F1 SC shoes weren't run-flats, though, so a small inflator was provided for emergencies. The new rolling stock and other slenderizing measures shaved nearly 50 pounds from curb weight. Cosmetic alterations were subtle: mesh grille inserts, red-painted brake calipers, a functional brake-cooling duct ahead of each rear wheel, and an arresting black-and-red interior with more heavily bolstered seats.

The Z06 proved a world-class performer in most every way. *Car and*

2000 C5 CORVETTE PRODUCTION CAR

2000 C5-R CORVETTE RACE CAR

Both pages: Y2K Corvettes received a number of detail changes as Chevy continued to strive for perfection. Sales continued the upward trend begun in 1998, as model-year production totaled 33,682 units. *Opposite, inset:* The C5 returned Corvette to big-league endurance racing in 1999. The factory-sponsored C5-R used a number of street-model components but also ultralight, high-tech carbon-fiber body panels and a greatly modified LS1 V-8 making 600 horsepower. The car showed its potential by placing 3rd in the GTS Class at the Rolex 24 Hours of Daytona.

Driver reported 0–60 at just 4.3 seconds, a heroic 0.98g of skidpad grip and "beautiful balance and great stability" on the track. Yet the Z06 was also surprisingly civilized on the street. All this for $43,855, just $500 more than a 'Vette ragtop. "When we recall that the old ZR-1 cost about twice as much as a garden-variety Corvette," *C/D* concluded, "[the Z06 is] a bargain...."

Total 'Vette production improved to 35,627 for model-year '01, but the 5773 souls who bought Z06s were doubtless peeved by the even hotter 2002 edition. Further honing lifted LS6 outputs to ZR-1 levels—405 hp, 400 pound-feet—and the suspension was again retuned for even racier handling and a less-agitated rough-road ride. Chevy said some of these improvements weren't ready in time for '01, so those who waited were amply rewarded. Total Corvette sales inched up to 35,767, but Z06 orders zoomed to 8297.

A production retreat to 35,469 units (including 8635 Z06s and

Opposite, top right: The racing C5-Rs got a 620-hp 7.0-liter engine for the 2000 campaign. Two cars finished an impressive 3rd and 4th in class and 10-11 overall in the prestigious 24 Hours of Le Mans. The 2001 season saw an outright win at the Daytona 24 Hours, a double-podium finish at Sebring, and a 1-2 GTS-class finish at Le Mans. *Other photos:* Chevy made the hardtop a more hardcore performer with the 2001 Z06. Boasting a specific LS6 V-8 with an extra 40 horses, plus an upgraded chassis and manual gearbox, it could run 0–60 mph in just 4.3 seconds and pull a neck-straining 0.98g on the skidpad. Cosmetic alterations were subtle and few.

14,022 ragtops) was a small downer for Corvette's 50th birthday year, but 2003 did bring developments worth celebrating. Besides commemorative insignia for all models, the convertible and hatchback offered an optional 50th Anniversary Package announced by special red paint, champagne-colored wheels, and unique trim. It looked expensive at $5000 but also included a new suspension trick called Magnetic Selective Ride Control. An innovation shared with Cadillac, MSRC used shock absorbers filled with a special fluid containing tiny metal particles. When acted on by an electric current, this "magnetorheological" fluid could change viscosity—thus damping firmness—in the blink of an eye. A suspension computer determined the appropriate damping rate based on sensor data on suspension movement, steering angle, and other variables. Drivers could select "Tour" or firmer "Sport" modes to suit road conditions. Judged highly effective in most magazine tests, MSRC was also a freestanding option for base models at a reasonable $1695. Finally, the coupe and convertible were upgraded to standard foglamps, sport seats, and dual-zone climate control. The Z06 was largely a carryover. Base prices crept up to $43,255 for the coupe, $49,700 for the ragtop, $50,485 for the Z06.

Both pages: Most Corvette news for 2002 involved the Z06, but the hatchback coupe remained the most popular model despite no major changes. Listing that year for $41,450, it again represented terrific high-performance value. The next best-selling model, the convertible, started at $47,975 for '02. The Z06 jumped to $50,150 but posted a 44-percent sales increase, with 8297. Among its many changes were a refined suspension, up-graded brakes, a newly standard head-up information display, and a bump to 405 horsepower, good for claimed 0–60 dashes of 3.9 sec-onds—quicker than the late, great ZR-1.

The C5 did well to hold its existing sales level, as it now faced a raft of new rivals bracketing its price range: a redesigned V-10 Dodge Viper, Nissan's V-6-powered 350Z, and Mazda's rotary-engine RX-8. And Porsche's mid-engine Boxster, though just as old as the C5 design, remained a formidable foe at prices that almost exactly duplicated the 'Vette's.

By now, though, the rumor mill had long been abuzz about the successor C6, and Chevy signaled a changing of the guard with Commemorative Edition packages as Corvette's main news for 2004. The title referred not to the C5's imminent departure but to a sterling 2003 racing season for the factory C5-Rs, which notched a third straight manufacturer's title in the American Le Mans Series after just missing a "three-peat" at the Le Mans 24 Hours. The Commemorative Packages must have been good luck, because C5-Rs won every race they entered in 2004, nabbing a fourth ALMS crown and an unprecedented third double victory in France (first in class and first overall).

There were two Commemorative packages: a $3700 ensemble for the coupe and convertible, and a more elaborate $4335 kit for the Z06. Both delivered vivid Le Mans Blue paint with wide, contrasting red-edged silver stripes on the hood, roof, and rear deck. Special "Le Mans 24 Hours" cross-flag emblems appeared on the nose and tail, and as embroidered logos on the headrests within a specific shale-colored cockpit. Polished alloy wheels completed the option, which also included all features of the Preferred Equipment Group.

To this, the Z06 package added a unique carbon-fiber hood taking a useful 10.6 pounds off the nose, plus special clearcoat-finish wheels with hubs reading "Commemorative 24:00 Heures du Mans." Moreover, testing on Germany's fabled Nürburgring prompted recalibrated shock absorbers and suspension bushes. These tweaks aimed to "settle" the car more quickly in fast transitions—and they did. *Car and Driver* praised the Commemorative Z06 for "steering response [now] so much quicker it's

Both pages: Corvette turned a half-century young with model-year 2003. All models got appropriate front-fender badges. Chevy also celebrated with a 50th Anniversary package that brought specific red paint, champagne-colored wheels, and an off-white "shale" interior with embroidered emblems. Also included was GM's new Magnetic Selective Ride Control, which mainly involved shock absorbers with a special fluid that changed viscosity, and thus firmness, as instructed by a suspension computer. Chevy built 4085 50th Anniversary coupes and 7547 convertibles; the option wasn't available with the hot Z06.

hard to believe the ratio is the same [as other Corvettes']. Its weight is within 141 pounds [of theirs], yet it feels like hundreds less. Its structure also feels twice as rigid." Another Commemorative Z06 proved the fastest stock Corvette ever tested by *Motor Trend,* clocking just 4.2 seconds 0–60 mph and a standing quarter-mile of 12.4 seconds at 117 mph.

Chevy followed tradition by limiting Commemorative production to 2026 Z06s, 2215 coupes, 2659 convertibles. Whatever one may think of "instant collector cars," these '04s were a fine send-off for a Corvette generation that was named 1998 North American Car of the Year, made *Car and Driver*'s "10 Best" list in 1999 and 2002–04, and earned perennial Consumer Guide® Best Buy honors.

But with the C6 awaiting in the wings, 2004 production slipped to 34,064 (including 5683 Z06s). After "only" eight years, it was time to move on once more.

Both pages: Corvette owners have personalized their cars for decades. Consider this 2004 "Z06" convertible. Chevrolet never offered such a car for sale, but that didn't stop this owner and several others from upgrading stock C5 ragtops. What Chevy did offer for 2004 was a trio of Commemorative Edition packages honoring the C5-R's third straight manufacturer's title win in the '03 American Le Mans series. The options also signaled the end of the C5 line after eight model years. All the Commemorative packages brought vivid Le Mans Blue paint with red-edged silver accents, "Le Mans 24 Hours" insignia inside and out, and a unique "shale" interior. The Z06 version added a lightweight carbon fiber hood and suspension tweaks divined in testing at Germany's famed Nürburgring racetrack.

2005-2011: HARD TIMES, GREAT CARS

The C6 was the first Corvette developed in concert with another General Motors car, the 2004 Cadillac XLR. Basically, it was a C5 with so many changes as to be 85 percent new by weight, according to Dave Hill, whose job title was now chief engineer for GM's Performance Car Group.

Team Corvette focused on 100 "dissatisfiers," things that needed fixing based on feedback from C5 owners and the team's own standards. Toward that end, lessons learned in making the XLR a world-class luxury tourer were applied to improving powertrain and road-noise isolation, interior execution, and overall workmanship. Yet the C6 was also developed with an eye to a racing C6-R, so ideas flowed freely between the Corvette Racing group and the production-car team.

With Tad Jeuchter as assistant chief engineer and Tom Peters as

head designer, the C6 emerged five inches shorter and an inch narrower than the C5 (at 174.6 and 72.6, respectively) on a wheelbase stretched 1.2 inches to 106. The last was dictated by XLR requirements but enhanced a purposeful new "wheels at the corners" stance. The wheels themselves were larger, now 18 inches in front and 19 in back.

Exposed headlamps—the first since 1962—saved weight and made aerodynamics fractionally slicker. Peters also restored a "port" grille (a slim air intake at the base of the nose); increased the "double bubble" contour of the coupe's liftoff roof panel; and applied a subtle "boattail" decklid line to both coupe and convertible. None of the composite body panels was left untouched, and an adept blend of curves and creases made for a leaner, more-muscular look.

The cockpit was also heavily revamped, gaining a simplified dashboard, more-convenient minor controls, aluminum and metal-look accents, larger new seats, even proper cupholders. A $1400 navigation system arrived as a first-time option, and new touch-activated electric door latches (with mechanical inside releases) were part of a standard keyless entry system with pocket transmitter and engine-start button, a "gift" from the XLR.

That button fired up a Chevy small-block V-8 so thoroughly modified as to warrant the new tag LS2. A 0.10-inch bore stretch (to 4.00 inches) upped displacement to 6.0 liters—364 cubes. Engineers also specified higher compression (10.9:1 vs. 10.1:1), redesigned high-flow intake and exhaust systems, and various internal changes that reduced pumping losses. Icing the cake, the LS2 was 15 pounds lighter than the LS1, helped by a new aluminum oil pan providing superior lubrication despite a quarter less capacity. With all this, the LS2 made an impressive 400 horsepower—just five horses shy of C5 Z06 output—and 400 pound-feet peak torque.

As before, transmissions comprised a six-speed Tremec T56 manual and four-speed GM automatic, both still rear-mounted. A revised linkage made manual shifting more positive, while the automatic got Cadillac-style shift programming. A six-speed automatic would replace it for 2006.

Though the C5's "Uniframe" was already quite stiff, the C6 benefited from extruded-aluminum members that were bolted and bonded to strengthen the door-hinge pillars. An underdash brace made of hydroformed steel, like the chassis siderails, tied those pillars more solidly to the

Opposite, top: C6 design work began late in 1999 and was essentially complete by fall 2001. Chevy PR released this "teaser" sketch shortly before the car's formal debut. This time the hatch coupe and convertible would bow together. *Opposite, bottom:* The C6 retained the C5's basic "performance vehicle architecture" with front-engine/rear-transaxle powertrain layout, but was 85 percent new by weight. Trimmer size, fewer pounds, and slicker aerodynamics were early-day goals that drove many design and engineering decisions. *This page, above:* The C6 cockpit was ergonomically superior to the C5's and showed the best workmanship in Corvette history. *Right and above right:* The Z06 returned for 2006 with a unique, high-tech *aluminum* structure and a 7.0-liter LS7 V-8 making 505 horsepower. The burly "427" engine was based on the new 6.0-liter/364-cid LS2 small-block that delivered 400 hp in regular 'Vettes.

central chassis tunnel. Ragtops gained extra rigidity from a fiberglass tub that not only served as the trunk but provided a rear cockpit wall lacking on the C5. Also new was an optional $1995 power top with hardware that weighed just 15 pounds and took up no more trunk space than the manual roof. The top itself was fully lined and reshaped to reduce wind noise.

Chassis changes were extensive. Though unchanged in design, the all-independent suspension featured all-new components, highlighted by shock absorbers with longer stroke for increased wheel travel, plus stiffer sway-bar mounts, revised bushings, and recalibrated springs. The base FE1 suspension adopted Goodyear's new-generation Eagle F1 GS run-flat tires. So did the Magnetic Ride Control option, repriced to $1695. The handling-focused Z51 Performance Package, now at $1495, substituted asymmetric-

Opposite and above: The C6 sported Corvette's first exposed headlamps since 1962, a change that saved pounds and reduced speed-sapping air drag. *Above:* Though clearly styled in the Corvette tradition, the C6 had a more chiseled appearance than the C5. Chief designer Tom Peters drew inspiration from both the classic 1963 Sting Ray split-window coupe and the angular Lockheed-Martin F/A-22 Raptor fighter jet. *Right:* Chevy's Corvette Racing arm worked side-by-side with the production C6 team to create a new C6-R racer. Based on the latest Z06, it would claim four straight American Le Mans Series team and manufacturer titles (2005-08) and three class victories at the 24 Hours of Le Mans.

tread Eagle F1 Supercar shoes in the same EEE sizes: P245/40ZR18 front, P285/35ZR19 rear. All C6s sported larger brakes but retained standard Active Handling traction/antiskid control.

Options were more extensive than ever: torso side airbags for coupes (newly standard for ragtops), GM's OnStar emergency-and-assistance service, satellite radio, and various packages with niceties like perforated leather upholstery, heated power seats and power telescopic steering column. Yet for all the many improvements, C6s cost little more than the final C5s. The convertible went up less than $1000, to $51,445, while the coupe stood pat at $43,710.

Unsurprisingly, the C6 got rave reviews. *Road & Track,* for example, ranked it first in a nine-way sports-car showdown for possessing "world-class performance, a high level of comfort and dashing good looks. And it's available for nearly half the price of a Porsche [911] Carrera S...America's sports car is now back in its rightful place atop the sports car mountain."

The C6 was passed over as 2005 North American Car of the Year, but it wasn't for lack of performance. Published road tests showed 0–60 mph in as little as 4.1 seconds, standing quarter-miles as low as 12.6 seconds at 114 mph, and trackworthy skidpad grip of 0.98g with the Z51 package. Yet real-world fuel economy was in the family sedan league at 18–20 mpg. "If you like your sports cars bold and brawny," Consumer Guide® summed up, "there's no better high-performance value." All considered though, model-year production of 37,372 units was slightly disappointing, being just 1381 units ahead of 2004.

After launching the coupe and convertible together for a change, Chevrolet unleashed a new Z06 as an early '06 model. Incorporating lessons from the C-5R racers, the C6 version was based on the fastback coupe, which had better high-speed aerodynamics than the previous notchback. A fixed roof panel was specified for extra rigidity. Even more significant, the Z06 was treated to a lighter, reengineered *aluminum* uniframe that more than offset the glassy fastback's greater weight. "It's

Opposite and near right: The C6 Z06 came only as a hatchback coupe with a fixed roof panel for extra high-speed rigidity. Other distinctions included a center nasal air intake, a deeper "port" grille above an aerodynamic splitter, and visibly bulged fenders—with the fronts made of carbon fiber. *Other photos this page:* Corvettes were now almost the default choice for Indy 500 pace-car duty. A C6 coupe served for 2005, a Z06 for '06, but no replicas were issued. The next year, though, saw 500 copies of this pace-car convertible—minus the special rear-facing lights mounted in the headrests.

like a whole different car," proclaimed Dave Hill. "It was an extremely large stretch to take 136 pounds out of something that only weighed about 350 to begin with . . . ." Also minimizing mass were a magnesium engine cradle (replacing an aluminum piece) and the use of carbon fiber for the floorboard skins and noticeably bulged fenders.

Under the Z06 hood was a new LS7 V-8 packing 505 hp and 470 pound-feet of torque. Though sized like the big-blocks of yore—7.0 liters, 427.6 cid—this pushrod powerhouse used the same "Gen IV" small-block architecture as the LS2, yet differed in most every respect: forged-steel crank, flat-top forged pistons giving 11.0:1 compression, sodium-filled exhaust valves, high-lift cam, racing-style dry-sump lubrication, specific low-restriction intake and exhaust. Yet for all the primo hardware, *Car and Driver* found that the "genius [in the LS7] is in the details, with careful attention paid to maximum airflow and valvetrain [lightness] and stiffness. The result is a big engine that revs like a small one . . . ."

Like its predecessor, the C6 Z06 came only with a six-speed manual gearbox, plus power-handling upgrades to the clutch, U-joints, rear halfshafts, and limited-slip differential. Brakes were also beefed up, with huge cross-drilled rotors of 14 inches fore and 13 aft clamped by six-piston front calipers and four-pot rears, all painted bright Corvette Red. Wheel diameters were C6 stock, but rim widths were increased to accommodate wider run-flat tires: 275/35 front, 325/30 rear. Other visual distinctions included a working cold-air scoop in the nose, radiused rear wheel openings, a wider grille, an air "splitter" below it, a small brake-cooling duct ahead of each rear wheel, and deeper, aero-enhancing perimeter body skirts. Interior changes were confined to two-toning, a slightly smaller steering wheel, and different seats with larger, nonadjustable bolsters.

Though it bowed at a stiff $70,000 before options, the C6 Z06 was an incredible buy in ultra-high performance. Some reviewers thought at-limit handling a tad nervous on the racetrack, but most found the car

Opposite: A 2008 Corvette highlight was the 427 Limited Edition Z06, a package option (RPO Z44) that paid homage to big-block 'Vettes of the 1960s. Alterations were strictly cosmetic: special wheels, red paint and interior, "427" insignia inside and out, and "stinger" hood graphics. Copies were capped at 505, of which 427 were marked for sale in the U.S. and Canada. *This page:* Base 2008 'Vettes like this convertible exchanged their LS2 V-8 for a bored-out and retuned LS3 engine making 430 hp from 6.2 liters (376 cubes). Corvette calendar-year sales plunged 20 percent from 2007 as the end of a national housing boom triggered the worst recession since the Thirties, a situation that magnified long-standing financial problems that forced General Motors to seek bankruptcy protection in 2009.

very well balanced on public roads. Acceleration was predictably fierce. *Car and Driver*'s tester "ripped to 60 mph in only 3.6 seconds, hit 100 in 7.9 and 150 in 17.5. That's on par with or better than the performance of the $153,345 Ford GT [and] $180,785 Ferrari F430.... When you experience this thrilling car...it seems reasonable to say that we're in the golden age of Corvette."

Base Corvettes were predictably little-changed for 2006 save one major improvement: a new six-speed automatic transmission with steering-wheel shift paddles to replace the previous four-speed option. Model-year production eased to 34,021, of which 6272 were Z06s. However, North American *calendar-year sales* rose 3805 units to 37,547.

The C6 Z06 had all the earmarks of a street-legal racing car. And indeed, it was the basis for the factory-backed Corvette Racing operation's newest endurance racer. The C6-R fast compiled an impressive record, starting with class wins in every race it ran in the 2005 American Le Mans

Series. It would go on to claim no fewer than four consecutive ALMS GT1 team and manufacturer's titles (2005–08) and three class victories at the 24 Hours of Le Mans (2005, 2006, 2009, bringing Corvette's total there to six). With little left to prove—and with most competitors starting to abandon GT1—Corvette Racing turned to the less-specialized but more-competitive GT2 class (later renamed GT) starting in 2009. More on that later.

Corvette continued to make pace-car appearances at the Indy 500. The C5 took its final tour in 2004 with actor Morgan Freeman at the wheel. A new C6 followed, piloted by General Colin Powell. A Z06 did the honors in 2006, helmed by world cycling champion Lance Armstrong, and a convertible was chosen for '07, driven by actor Patrick Dempsey. Tellingly, all these cars were mechanically close to stock, having more than enough muscle to pace the field, but only the '07 ragtop was offered as a retail replica: 500 copies that, oddly enough, were all but unadvertised.

Both pages: Though it had all the hallmarks of a street-legal racing car, the C6 Z06 was a surprisingly tractable and comfortable daily driver. Practical, too, as it boasted the same class-leading XXL trunk space as the regular hatch coupe. Even so, it had acceleration that matched or beat that of much pricier "exotics" like the Ford GT. After clocking 0-60 mph in just 3.6 seconds and 0-100 in a mere 7.9, the Z06 was described by one magazine as "a thrilling car" symbolizing a new "golden age of Corvette."

The likely reason is that 2007 was a mostly carryover Corvette year and big changes were just ahead. Those began with yet another evolution of the classic small-block V-8 for 2008 base models. Designated LS3, this was essentially an LS2 bored-out by 0.06-inch to displace 6.2 liters or 376 cid. Engineers also applied high-flow fuel injectors from the LS7 Z06 engine, plus larger valves in freer-breathing cylinder heads. Despite slightly lower compression to accommodate cleaner-burning E85 ethanol-blended fuel, the LS3 produced 430 hp and 424 pound-feet of torque in standard tune; an optional "dual-mode" exhaust system upped the counts to 436 and 428, respectively. In addition, all '08 'Vettes got a more-precise manual-shift linkage and revised steering with a more-natural feel and improved componentry. Though little faster or grippier than earlier base C6s, the '08 was easier to drive *in extremis*. Considering its go-power, it was remarkably thrifty too, Consumer Guide® recording 17.7 mpg in city/highway driving and nearly 22 with mostly open-road work.

Corvette returned to The Brickyard in 2008 for its 10th pace-car outing, and Chevy made a big deal of it, issuing 500 LS3-powered replicas with striking silver-and-black livery recalling the first Corvette pace car of 30 years before. Priced as separate models for a change, these coupes and convertibles cost about $5000 more than standard—$58,240 and $67,310, respectively—but that included the Z51 handling package, dual-mode exhaust, head-up display, and other amenities. Also added to the 2008 lineup was the 427 Limited Edition Z06, an $83,345 head-turner featuring red "tintcoat" metallic paint, unique graphics evoking the "stinger" hood of big-block '67 Sting Rays, and additional creature comforts. Production was capped at 505, matching Z06 horsepower, with 78 copies earmarked for export.

By now, though, the U.S. economy was in free fall as the country's housing boom went bust, and not even Corvette could outrun the new "Great Recession." Calendar-year sales plunged 20 percent from '07 to 26,971, then fell to barely half that in 2009—13,934—when General Motors

Opposite and this page, above and right:
Despite the start of economic "hard times" in 2008, Chevrolet unleashed the most potent and priciest showroom Corvette ever. An early '09 intro reviving the ZR1 name (without a hyphen), it ran with a handbuilt *supercharged* 6.2-liter LS9 V-8 packing a massive 638 horsepower. Unique ultralight carbon-fiber body panels included a "see-through" hood revealing the supercharger's intercooler. Price: nearly $104,000. *Right:* Corvette racing ran new ZR1-based C6-Rs in 2009 GT2-class competition, but claimed only a few top-five finishes.

was forced to do the unthinkable and declare bankruptcy in exchange for a taxpayer-funded bailout.

How ironic, then, that the costliest, most potent Corvette ever was announced in early '08 for model-year 2009. Reviving the hallowed ZR1 moniker—without a hyphen—it was not unexpected, having been rumored for at least two years as project "Blue Devil" (a nod to GM's then-CEO and Duke University alum Rick Wagoner).

The headline attraction was a handbuilt *supercharged* 6.2 V-8 labeled LS9 and certified for 638 hp and 604 pound-feet of torque. Installed in the fixed-roof, aluminum-frame Z06 structure, it linked to a mandatory six-speed manual gearbox with a dual-disc clutch that was specified to cope with the massive power but also made routine driving even easier than in a Z06. To maximize the muscle, Team Corvette rendered the hood, front fenders, roof panel, roof bow, front splitter, and rocker panels in ultralight

carbon fiber instead of thermoplastic. The result was a commendable base curb weight of 3324 pounds, less than 100 more than the base coupe. Chassis upgrades included a specially tuned version of Corvette's Magnetic Selective Ride Control suspension, exotic carbon-ceramic Brembo-brand disc brakes with larger rotors (15.5 inches fore, 15.0 aft), and specific Michelin Pilot Sport 2 tires massively sized at P285/30ZR19 front and P335/25ZR20 rear.

Many critics complained that ZR1 interior distinctions were limited to logos on the seats and a boost gauge. Exterior bling was more plentiful: wider front fenders with functional twin air ducts, a specific decklid spoiler, four center-mount exhaust pipes and—the real eye-grabber—a polycarbonate window in the hood to show off the blower's intercooler.

As the new ultimate Corvette and being so highly specialized, the ZR1 was predictably expensive: $103,970 to start. Options were limited

Opposite: A welcome antidote to the bad economic news of 2009 was Chevy's newest concept Corvette: Stingray. It was a mean-looking machine that many viewed as a forecast of the next-generation 'Vette. Actually, the Stingray was created for a starring role in that year's CGI epic, *Transformers: Revenge of the Fallen. This page:* The ZR1 was as close to a factory custom as Chevy had ever offered. Although it was the priciest Corvette in history, it was also a world-class sizzler that could outperform certain Ferraris costing three times as much.

to a 3ZR package of comfort and convenience amenities priced at a cool $10,000, plus chrome wheels at $2000. But pricey though it was, the ZR1 was another Corvette that outperformed much-costlier import-brand rivals. *Motor Trend* recorded such sizzling stats as 0–60 mph in 3.3 seconds, an 11.2-second quarter-mile at 130.5 mph, and skidpad stick of 1.10g. "Performance-wise, the ZR1 trumps the [Ferrari] 599 GTB in almost every objective category. It's also about one-third [the price]." Some things never change.

Chevy announced that ZR1 production would be limited to about 2000 a year, but it's doubtful that many were built for '09, a difficult model year that brought virtually no changes to base and Z06 versions. August 2009 saw the debut of the planned ZR1-based C6-R ALMS endurance racer, but it managed only a few top-five GT-class finishes before finally notching an outright victory at the 2010 season finale at Road Atlanta.

Meantime, Corvette sales withered to a modern low in calendar 2010: just 12,624 units. But news on other fronts gave cause for celebration.

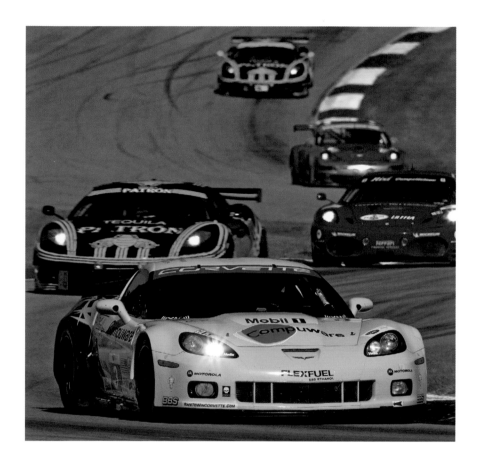

Above: After dominating the GT1 class in the American Le Mans Series, Corvette Racing and other teams refocused on the GT2 class starting in 2009. Later named GT, this category allowed fewer modifications from stock, which made for closer, more exciting competition. *Other photos:* Announced at the same time as production of the 1.5 millionth Corvette was the new 2010 Grand Sport. It was available in convertible and coupe versions, combining the base LS3 powertrain with the Z06's wide-track chassis and special trim inside and out.

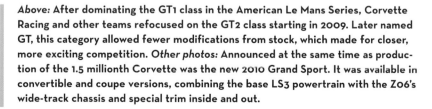

For starters, GM roared back from bankruptcy as a much leaner and financially healthier automaker with fresh products that people actually bought in strong numbers. As a result, the reorganized General Motors *Company* posted 21-percent higher North American sales in 2010 and was making money for the first time in years.

More important to our story, the C6 kept on getting better. The big development for 2010 was the Grand Sport coupe and convertible, an appealing combination of the LS3 powertrain and the Z06's wide-track chassis and styling features. Respective prices were $54,770 and $58,550, about $5000–$6000 above base-trim counterparts. A replacement for the Z51 package, the GS ensemble included a numerically higher performance

Opposite top: The ZR1-based C6-R scored is first overall GT-class American Le Mans Series victory in the 2010 season finale at Road Atlanta. *Opposite bottom and this page:* The new-for-2010 Grand Sport models cost some $5000-$6000 more than base-trim versions, but offered excellent value. Standards included a special handling suspension, tighter final-drive ratio, and upgraded cooling system, brakes, and tires. A Z06-style hood with functional air intake was also part of the package, as was a performance-enhancing launch-control function with manual transmission. Contrasting front-fender hash marks were among the options.

axle ratio, sport suspension, uprated cooling system and brakes, wider tires, and special trim. In addition, all "manny tranny" 2010s gained GM's new Launch Control, a performance-enhancing add-on to the standard stability system that modulated engine speed to maximize grip during full-throttle launches. The ZR1 also got a "Performance Traction Management" system that automatically adjusted the traction control and suspension firmness to suit high-performance driving.

Further refinements marked the 2011 lineup. Base and GS models got larger cross-drilled brake rotors, and Magnetic Ride Control was a new GS option. The ZR1 was largely a rerun, but the Z06 offered a new Z07 Performance Package that bundled the MRC with Brembo-brand ceramic brakes and larger tires on unique 20-spoke wheels. Also new was a Z06 Carbon Fiber Package with a lightweight roof panel and lower-body skirts *a la* ZR1. This formed the basis for a planned 500-unit run of Z06 Carbon models with specific trim and a unique bulged carbon-fiber hood.

That's the Corvette story so far, but there's surely more to come. After all, the "Great Recession" must end sooner or later, and GM's new and much-improved competitiveness bodes well for Corvette's survival.

As for what lies ahead, it's believed the C7 will arrive for 2013 as a lighter, more-aerodynamic take on the stalwart C6, followed five years later by a C8 that could be the mid-engine design Corvette fans have been dreaming of for decades. We can't wait.

Opposite: Base Corvettes were little changed for 2011, and were no less appealing for that. The C6 coupe's "double-bubble" roof contour and "boattail" rear-deck shape are evident here. By this time, a leaner, post-bankruptcy General Motors was scoring much stronger sales and its first profits in years, all of which bode well for the future of America's sports car. *This page:* ZR1 remained the most powerful Corvette for 2011, but the Z06 was newly available with an optional Carbon package limited to just 500 copies. Priced at $3995, it delivered the ZR1's lightweight carbon-fiber body panels and big, lacy-spoke wheels.

INDEX